The Account Which We Must Give

Studies on The Judgment Seat of Christ

Other Books by Carl G. Johnson

52 Story Telling Programs
More Story Telling Programs
Miracles and Melodies Story Telling Programs
Special Occasion Sermon Outlines
Preaching Helps
Preaching Truths for Perilous Times
My Favorite Illustrations
My Favorite Outlines
Ready for Anything
Hell You Say!
Prophecy Made Plain for Times like These
Is the Bible Full of Contradictions?
101 True Stories for Children

The Account Which We Must Give

Studies on The Judgment Seat of Christ

Carl G. Johnson

REGULAR BAPTIST PRESS
1300 North Meacham Road
Schaumburg, Illinois 60173–4888

Library of Congress Cataloging-in-Publication Data

Johnson, Carl G.
   The account which we must give : studies on the judgment seat of Christ / Carl
G. Johnson
        p.   cm.
   Includes bibliographical references.
   ISBN 0–87227–140–4
      1. Judgment Day. 2. Christian ethics—Baptist authors. 3. Conscience, Exami-
nation of. 4. Second Advent.   I. Title.
BT882.J64
236'.9—dc20   90–34224
                                                                             CIP

THE ACCOUNT WHICH WE MUST GIVE
© 1990
Regular Baptist Press
Schaumburg, Illinois 60173–4888

Second printing—1991

A C K N O W L E D G M E N T S

We acknowledge with appreciation the quotations taken from *CHRISTIAN THEOLOGY* by Emery H. Bancroft. Copyright 1976 by Baptist Bible College. Used by permission of Zondervan Publishing House; *PROFILES IN PROPHECY* by S. Franklin Logsdon. Copyright 1964 by S. Franklin Logsdon, copyright 1970 by Zondervan Publishing House. Used by permission; *THE RETURN OF THE LORD* by John F. Walvoord. Copyright 1955 by Dunham Publishing Company. Used by permission of Zondervan Publishing House; *THINGS TO COME* by J. Dwight Pentecost. Copyright 1958 by Dunham Publishing Company, copyright 1986 by Zondervan Publishing House. Used by permission.

We acknowledge the quotations taken from "THE JUDGMENT SEAT OF CHRIST" by Thomas M. Meachum in *BIBLICAL VIEWPOINT*, Copyright 1977, Bob Jones University, Greenville, South Carolina. Used by permission.

We also acknowledge quotations from *THE JUDGMENT SEAT OF CHRIST* by Martin R. De Haan, M.D., Copyright 1951, Radio Bible Class, Grand Rapids, Michigan. Used by permission.

C O N T E N T S

FOREWORD

The Account Which We Must Give is a sobering book. Careless Christians and slipshod saints will read it with much profit. God has given all believers definite responsibilities, and He will require specific accountability at the Judgment Seat of Christ. Brother Johnson's work is certainly a great motivation to holiness of life. *The Account Which We Must Give* is a Biblically balanced book. The author treats the subjects of reward and loss with Scriptural clarity and conviction. He does not give in to the temptation to speculate but stays strictly with Biblical data. He does not avoid the more difficult passages having to do with the Judgment Seat of Christ but includes what the Bible has to say about tears in Heaven, the five crowns, the bride making herself ready and the Judge Himself.

Such complete treatment of the Judgment Seat of Christ is hard to find in one volume. Brother Johnson has given us a work that will awaken our consciences, stir us to lives of obedient service and cause us to want to please our Lord Jesus Christ, our Heavenly Bridegroom. I highly commend and enthusiastically recommend this valuable volume.

PAUL N. TASSELL, PH.D., LITT. D.

National Representative of the General Association
of Regular Baptist Churches

I once read this statement by Leonard Ravenhill:

> Is there then a forgotten truth from the holy and imperishable word of the living God that could shake this Laodicean Church from its creeping paralysis? I believe there is. If there is no word from the Lord in this hour, there certainly is no word for the Church from anyone else. One day I grasped two handfuls of books of sermons and found that not one of them had a message on the judgment seat of Christ. This, I am persuaded after much thought, is the most neglected part of eschatology. Sermons there are and books without number on the Second Coming of Christ, but books dealing as a sole subject with the judgment seat of Christ can be counted on one hand. Why is this? Does meditation on such a penetrating truth terrify the minister? Well it might.
>
> Unsupported by friend, wife, or attorney, each of us must one day stand before Jehovah's awful throne.[1]

Dr. John A. Sproule, writing in *Spire,* said, "To my knowledge, there is no substantial work, produced by those who hold to a dispensational theology, dealing with the negative aspect of the *Bēma* [judgment seat]."[2]

These two statements caused me to think and study to see what God says about the Judgment Seat of Christ. In my months of study I found only two small paperback books on the subject, although I searched through literally hundreds of Christian books and booklets. I checked *Biblical Viewpoint,* a magazine published by Bob Jones University, starting with Volume 1, No. 1, April 1967, through Volume XX, No. 2, November 1986, and found only one article, written by Thomas M. Meachum, in Volume XI, No. 1, April 1977. I went through the issues of *Bibliotheca Sacra,* a quarterly published by Dallas Theological Seminary, from 1934 to 1980, and found only three articles—one by Dr. John F. Walvoord in 1966, and two by Samuel L. Hoyt in 1980. Most of the books I looked at, either prophetic books or books commenting on the three main passages in the New Testament dealing with the

Judgment Seat of Christ (Rom. 14:10; 1 Cor. 3:9–15; 2 Cor. 5:10), did not give any help on this important truth.

I agree with Leonard Ravenhill that this is the most neglected part of eschatology. Dr. Walvoord said, "There is no more practical prophetic truth than this simple pointed doctrine of the judgment seat of Christ."[3] An English prophetic scholar wrote of this judgment: "Here too is a thought that *should* be the greatest inducement to holy living, greater than any other single thing."[4]

Dr. Merrill F. Unger commented:

> The doctrine of the believer's judgment is a definite teaching of the inspired oracles. It is a vital part of the divine revelation.
>
> It would not be easy to find another scriptural truth, at once so vital and pivotal to practical Christian living, subject to so much disregard and error.

Dr. J. Dwight Pentecost saw the importance of this truth: "There are few doctrines of greater importance to the child of God than the doctrine of the Judgment Seat of Christ."[5]

St. Augustine tells how this truth affected his life: "Nothing has contributed more powerfully to wean me from all that held me down to earth than the thought constantly dwelt on of death and of the last account."[6]

Dr. A. W. Tozer wrote of the Judgment Seat of Christ:

> Throughout the Christian church as we know it today, all sense of accountability to God seems to have been lost. Christians no longer sing with very much feeling that hymn of Charles Wesley's that asks our Lord to
>
> "Arm me with jealous care
> As in Thy sight to live;
> And Oh, Thy servant, Lord, prepare
> A strict account to give."
>
> Someone has been quoted recently as saying: "If I believed that I had to give an accounting of my service as seen in the eyes of God, I could never be happy!"

The quality of our Christian life is sure to be affected if we do not feel that we are going to give an account to God of how we have used the time, abilities, money and possessions He has entrusted to us.

The results of this time of testing will be seen in that great and coming day before the Judgment Seat of Christ. Someone has written that the Apostle Paul surely lived with one eye on the Judgment Seat of Christ and the other on the perishing world.[7]

In this book I have written—and included the writings of other men of God—on this most important subject. I have presented both the positive and negative aspects of the Judgment Seat of Christ, with the purpose of

. . . inciting believers to a life of holy, faithful service to the Lord Jesus Christ in view of a future day of accounting before the Lord. Chrysostom was right when he wrote that "men are not much influenced by the prospect of losing possible blessings; the dread of possible pains is more influential." What a transformation would take place in our churches if all of the awesomeness of the Judgment Seat of Christ were properly proclaimed.[8]

My prayer is that it has been properly proclaimed in this book.

Carl G. Johnson

THE ACCOUNT WHICH WE MUST GIVE

Daniel Webster was at one time considered the greatest of all living Americans. He was outstanding as a statesman, lawyer, orator and leader of men. Twenty-five national leaders attended a select banquet in his honor. One man at the banquet asked Mr. Webster, "Sir, what is the greatest thought that ever entered your mind?"

Without hesitation, Webster replied, "The greatest thought that ever entered my mind was the thought of my responsibility to God." As he spoke, he wept, excused himself from the banquet and went outside to get control of his emotions. When he returned, he talked for thirty minutes about man's responsibility to God.[1]

Yes, this is a great thought and it should enter our minds. We should make adequate preparation for that meeting with God. Jesus Christ will soon come back and reckon with us. God's sure Word says, "So then every one of us shall give account of himself to God" (Rom. 14:12).

THE SAINTS MUST GIVE ACCOUNT TO GOD

According to the Bible, all Christians will one day stand before the Judgment Seat of Christ to be judged according to the works they have done since they became Christians (Rom. 14:10; 1 Cor. 3:9–15; 2 Cor. 5:10).

... It is to God that we have to give account; each for himself

15

accounting, and not for another, unto Him that trieth the hearts. We may be sure that if our present thoughts of grace wherein we stand do not lead us into the presence of God, we are not in our true position. To have to do with God is our calling now. "Beloved, if our heart condemn us not, then have we confidence toward God. And whatsoever we ask, we receive of him, because we keep his commandments, and do those things that are pleasing in his sight" (I John 3:21–22). It is thus that an exercised heart and conscience make the prospect of appearing to give account to God a prospect of joy rather than of dread. . . . That they who judge themselves shall not be judged, is elsewhere laid down as a settled maxim of Divine government. But do we always judge ourselves? This is a question which each believer should often put to his own heart. For it cannot be doubted, that *neglected* sins, habitual and contented carelessness, with all that savours of high minded self-complacency, must show themselves again at that great day, to become fuel for the fire which will try the work of every man (I Cor. 3:13–15). So also will there then be called up, for a final hearing and decision, a multitude of questions, which in the long day of faith and patience, have divided saint from saint, and made, (to our shame it must be said), internal controversy to be a permanent condition of the Church. The question put in verse 10 of this chapter [Rom. 14] will not, until then, receive its perfect and conclusive answer. What we remember as penitents the Lord forgets; but He has a book of remembrance for all things, good or evil, which we have done and not repented, since we took His name as our own (II Cor. 5:8–10).[2]

PREACHERS MUST GIVE ACCOUNT TO GOD

God's Word says in Hebrews 13:17: "Obey them that have the rule over you, and submit yourselves: for they watch for your souls, as they that *must give account*. . . ." Comparing this verse with Hebrews 13:7, we find that when God speaks of "them which have the rule over you," He is primarily speaking of those "who have spoken unto you the word of God." What a great responsibility preachers have!

A young pastor of a little church complained to the "prince of preachers," Charles H. Spurgeon, about the smallness of his church and its few members. Spurgeon asked him, "How many members do you have?"

"Fifty," replied the young pastor.

"Ah," exclaimed Spurgeon, "that's more than you will want to account for on the Day of Judgment."

Evangelist John Linton made this statement in his message "Tears in Heaven":

> Here is a preacher, a saved man, but lacking in the courage that would make him stand firm in a day of compromise. He has not put first things first. He has surrendered some of the fundamentals of the faith. He has denied a literal hell. He has pooh-poohed the second coming of Christ. He has been silent on the new birth. He has received members into his church who are not saved, and in so doing has kept them from ever being saved. These church members through his compromise and cowardice are now in hell. He now stands before the Christ whose literal coming he denied. He learns of the souls lost through his disobedience. He stands revealed to all the Church and to himself as a place-seeker, a pleaser of men, a destroyer of souls. In the white light of the judgment seat how will that preacher feel? Will he shed no tears in heaven? What think ye?[3]

A story is told of a pastor in Hampshire who went through his ordinary weekly round of services but had no converts, nor expected any. One morning, as he came down to breakfast, his wife, noticing that he looked haggard and ill, asked him what was the matter.

"Oh," he said, "I've had a most awful dream."

"Dreams are nothing!" she replied.

"I don't know," he said. "There was something in this dream. I thought I was standing at Christ's judgment seat, and He looked me in the face and said, 'Where are the souls of the children I gave you?' "

" 'I do not know, Lord!' "

" 'Where are the souls of the servants who lived in your house?' "

" 'I don't know, Lord,' again I had to reply."

" 'Where are the souls of the congregation to whom I appointed you a minister?' "

"And I said: 'Oh, Lord, I know not; I never spoke to any of them!' "

"As I said these words, I seemed to sink into perdition, and I thought I was hunted through Hell by those lost souls—and I awoke."

As the clergyman said these words, he fell over against his wife—dead.

Isaac M. Haldeman made this statement concerning preachers:

> The preachers who in spite of the blindness and blundering of their wood, hay and stubble work have been really regenerated, have had some element of divine life; the foolish and deceived workers who have mistaken quantity for quality, will in that hour when they stand at the Judgment Seat of Christ be accused of unfaithfulness to their trust and shall suffer loss.[4]

Frederick L. Brooks recorded the following account:

> Mr. Spurgeon said that in his early ministry he received a great spiritual uplift by a strange revelation which came to him in a dream. He was sitting in his arm chair and fell asleep. As he slept, there came into the room a stranger bearing a pair of balances, a crucible, and a hammer. The stranger came toward him, and, extending his hand said, *"How is your heart?"* Spurgeon put his hand in his bosom and brought forth his heart and handed it to the stranger for inspection. He took it and placed it in his scales, weighing it carefully. Mr. Spurgeon heard him say, *"One hundred parts."* The stranger broke the mass into atoms, put it in his crucible, and put the crucible into the fire. When the mass had fused he took it out and set it down to cool. It congealed in cooking and formed into various layers. The stranger broke the layers apart and weighed each of them, taking notes as he worked. Finally, he handed to Mr. Spurgeon the result of his test: Total 100 Parts. Of this, in analysis; bigotry, 10 parts; personal ambition, 23 parts; love of praise, 19 parts; pride of denomination, 15 parts; pride of talents, 14 parts; love of authority,

12 parts; love to God, 4 parts; love to man, 3 parts. Only seven parts real! How frequently we need to search our hearts![5]

Thank God, it is possible for preachers to be rewarded at the Judgment Seat of Christ instead of suffering loss, because God's Word promises the preacher: "Feed the flock of God which is among you . . . and when the Chief Shepherd shall appear, ye shall receive a crown of glory that fadeth not away" (1 Pet. 5:2–4).

ALL CHRISTIANS MUST GIVE ACCOUNT TO GOD

God said in 2 Corinthians 5:10: "For we must all appear before the judgment seat of Christ; that every one may receive the things done in his body, according to that he hath done, whether it be good or bad." I believe if Christians understood and believed this truth, much of the loose living we see today among God's people would change, and we would live "with eternity's values in view."

> To be made manifest means not just to appear, but to be laid bare, stripped of every outward façade of respectability, and openly revealed in the full and true reality of one's character. All our hypocrisies and concealments, all our secret, intimate sins of thought and deed, will be open to the scrutiny of Christ—a clear indication, incidentally, of the absolute Deity of the Redeemer, for it is only the divine gaze which penetrates to the very essence of our personality: "man looketh on the outward appearance, but the Lord looketh on the heart" (I Sam. 16:7). The conduct of our lives should constantly be influenced by the solemn remembrance that "[there is no] creature that is not manifest in [God's] sight; but all things are naked and laid [open before] the eyes of him with whom we have to do" (Heb. 4:13; cf. I Cor. 4:5). In that day of manifestation both the hypocritical and the hypercritical will be shown for what they really are.[6]

At the Judgment Seat of Christ, where the Christian's life and works will be reviewed and examined, rewards will be given for faithfulness, and loss will be experienced for unfaithfulness (cf.

1 Cor. 3:9–15). We must give account of our time, our money, our words, our actions, our thoughts, our motives, our talents, our influence.

Dr. Robert T. Ketcham put it this way:

> What our eyes looked on, what our ears listened to, what our hearts loved, what our minds believed, what our lips said, what our hands did, where our feet walked, our secrets, our motives, and our decisions all come out under the fire of His holy eye. We will tell Him *all;* not only *what* we did but *why* we did it! In the light of that record we will receive "good" or "bad."[7]

Our lives before we were saved will not be brought up, thank God, for the Lord has not only forgiven our sins, but He has also forgotten them (1 John 2:12; Heb. 10:17). The sins we confess as children of God will not be brought up against us, because God promised in 1 John 1:9: "If we confess our sins, he is faithful and just to forgive us our sins, and to cleanse us from all unrighteousness." Dr. F. E. Marsh stated: "Sins confessed are sins forgiven."[8] But if our lives have been unfaithful and if we have unconfessed sins in our lives, we must face this judgment, and we will feel much shame (1 John 2:28).

Dr. Graham Scroggie once said, "I would rather go through the Great Tribulation than endure what I believe some Christians will go through at the Judgment Seat of Christ."[9]

Dr. William Culbertson, a former president of Moody Bible Institute, remarked:

> I'm sure that if there are tears to be shed at the judgment seat of Christ, some of us are going to weep out our hearts because of the opportunities we have allowed to slip away while we were looking for something bigger. Five minutes in the presence of Christ will make us wish we had spent more time in prayer, witnessing, and learning to help others down here. BUT THEN IT WILL BE TOO LATE.

Roy L. Laurin, in his book *Life Endures,* made this statement: "Here the believer must face unconfessed sin. Here he must adjust all the differences with fellow [believers] which were not settled in the flesh."[10]

Theodore H. Epp said:

> We were purchased with the redemptive blood of Christ and so we belong to Him (I Cor. 6:19, 20). We are not our own anymore. We are His to do with according to His will. Because of this, some difference in rewards must be made between the man who has totally given himself to the Lord and one who may have accepted salvation as an escape from hell. If this latter Christian did little or nothing to allow Christ to live in and through him so that others might know what Christ has done for him, he will not be worthy of rewards. The Lordship of the Lord Jesus is clearly evident in the one but is not nearly so evident in the other. No doubt, most of us would come in between those two extremes. But we see from this why the Judgment Seat of Christ is necessary. It will show how much each one has appropriated Christ's life and reflected that life here on the earth.[11]

Dr. W. H. Griffith Thomas, a well-known expositor of the Word of God, wrote:

> While a genuine Christian who becomes a backslider will not be judicially condemned forever, there *will* be a very serious measure of personal and *practical condemnation* when such an one stands before the judgment seat of Christ to be dealt with according to works since conversion.[12]

I again quote Dr. Ketcham:

> Brethren, have we overworked *grace?* Because we *must* be entirely passive under the blood for our *salvation,* have we concluded that we are not to be *active* in a life of service? Thanks be to His infinite *grace,* I am a child in my Father's family, *but* does not *that fact itself* force another—namely, that my Father has a right to deal with His child in corrective chastisement? And *will* He not do so *here,* and *if necessary,* hereafter?

Oh, that we might always *live* for eternity, *preach* for eternity, *pray* for eternity, and *work* for eternity, lest we be ashamed *away from before* Him at His coming . . . (1 John 2:28).[13]

Dr. H. H. Savage, in a message entitled, "What God Will Do with the Unfaithful," delivered at Moody Founder's Week Conference in 1962, unburdened his heart:

> I read books about the judgment seat of Christ by such men as Dr. M. R. DeHaan, Dr. Norman B. Harrison and Dr. H. A. Ironside, but I didn't agree with them. But now I have been looking at some Bible verses, and do you know, I rather think these men are right. Where there are things not right, it is going to be a terrible thing for Christians to face almighty God. . . .
>
> ". . . And again, The Lord shall judge his people. It is a fearful thing to fall into the hands of the living God" [Heb. 10:30, 31]. It will be fearful for those who are disobedient, those who refuse to be under His leadership and under His guidance and to do what He has asked them to do; it will be a fearful thing for disobedient, careless, indifferent Christians at that time.[14]

Then he told this incident:

> Fifty-one years ago, I lived here in the 153 building. I came home one night with a few others who had been walking around the block. I don't think we had been anywhere, just out strolling a bit. As I came in the front door I noticed Dr. R. A. Torrey was standing on the steps, and the fellow who went in ahead of me was in front of him.
>
> Dr. Torrey was an austere man. I was afraid of him in those days. He said something like this: "Where have you been?" "Oh, we've just been out walking." "Talk to anybody about the Lord?" "Well, Dr. Torrey, I didn't have an assignment tonight." "Assignment nothing. Weren't you assigned by the Lord?" "Well, maybe." "And you didn't talk to anybody? What have you been doing?" "Just walking around." "What good did that do you?" That poor fellow was sweating about that time. Do you know what I did? I went around the back and climbed up the fire escape.
>
> But there is no fire escape to climb up when you have to meet the

Lord. When He says, "What were you doing on earth? Were you true to Me? . . . You claimed to be wholly consecrated to Me; were you wholly consecrated?" What will you say? You will have to meet Him before the innumerable company of angels, and the Church of the firstborn, because these things will be made manifest and drawn out into the light.[5]

In the light of this tremendous truth and the fact that Jesus may come at any moment, we should "abide in him; that, when he shall appear, we may have confidence, and not be ashamed before him at his coming" (1 John 2:28). If we are true to Him, wholly consecrated to Him, obedient to Him, faithful to Him, walking in the Spirit, when He comes, He will say to us, "Well done, thou good and faithful servant: thou hast been faithful over a few things, I will make thee ruler over many things: enter thou into the joy of thy lord" (Matt. 25:21).

THE SINNERS MUST GIVE ACCOUNT TO GOD

God's Word is perfectly clear on this fact:

> And I saw a great white throne, and him that sat on it, from whose face the earth and the heaven fled away; and there was found no place for them. And I saw the dead, small and great, stand before God; and the books were opened: and another book was opened, which is the book of life: and the dead were judged out of those things which were written in the books, according to their works. And the sea gave up the dead which were in it; and death and hell delivered up the dead which were in them: and they were judged every man according to their works. And death and hell were cast into the lake of fire. This is the second death. And whosoever was not found written in the book of life was cast into the lake of fire (Rev. 20:11–15).

"And as it is appointed unto men once to die, but after this the judgment" (Heb. 9:27). "Because he hath appointed a day, in the which he will judge the world in righteousness by that man whom he hath ordained; whereof he hath given assurance unto all men,

23

in that he hath raised him from the dead" (Acts 17:31). "For God shall bring every work into judgment, with every secret thing, whether it be good, or whether it be evil" (Eccles. 12:14).

Every person who dies unsaved will one day be resurrected and stand before the Lord Jesus Christ for judgment at the Great White Throne, because, according to John 5:22, "The Father judgeth no man, but hath committed all judgment unto the Son." God has a record of every sinner's sins, every lie told, everything stolen, every dishonesty, every wicked thought and action, every evil word uttered, every secret sin.

J. A. Seiss, in his book *The Apocalypse,* said:

> . . . Not a human being has ever breathed earth's atmosphere whose career is not traced at full length in the book of eternity. Yes, O man! O woman! whoever you may be, your biography is written. An unerring hand has recorded every item, with every secret thing. There is not an ill thought, a mean act, a scene of wrong in all your history, a dirty transaction, a filthiness of speech, or a base feeling that ever found entertainment in your heart, but is there described in bold hand, by its true name, and set down to your account, to be then brought forth for final settlement, if not clean blotted out through faith in Christ's blood before this present life of yours is ended.[16]

But, thanks be to God, our sins can be "clean blotted out through faith in Christ's blood." Jesus promised: "Verily, verily, I say unto you, He that heareth my word, and believeth on him that sent me, hath everlasting life, and shall not come into condemnation; but is passed from death unto life" (John 5:24). When a sinner hears the Word of God, believes it and receives Jesus Christ as his personal Savior and Lord, he can rest on the Word of God, which assures him: "Believe on the Lord Jesus Christ, and thou shalt be saved, and thy house" (Acts 16:31). Then he can rejoice in the Word of God, which says, "He that believeth on him is not condemned" (John 3:18), and "There is therefore now no condemnation to them which are in Christ Jesus" (Rom. 8:1), and he "shall not come into condemnation [or judgment]" (John 5:24).

Daniel Curry was a mighty man of God in the Middle West. Once he had a dream that focused on the believer's rewards rather than on the issue of salvation. In his dream he ascended to Heaven and knocked on the gate. He was asked for his name and then was told that it could not be found but that if he wished, he could appear before the judgment throne and answer for himself. He was carried rapidly away until he came into the presence of a mighty, shining light. It was a million times brighter than anything he had ever seen on earth, and its brightness seemed to blind him. He could see nothing except the light, but soon he heard a voice out of the midst of it, saying, "Daniel Curry, have you always been good?"

He had to answer, "No."

"Have you always been pure?"

Again his answer was, "No."

"Have you always been charitable in your opinion of others?"

"I cannot say that I have been."

"Have you always been fair and precisely just in your dealings with your fellowmen?"

"No, I haven't been." And as he stood there thinking that the end would come any second, he heard a voice sweeter than the voice of any mother. As he turned, he saw One standing by his side with a face sweeter than any face he had ever seen on earth, and that voice of unspeakable sweetness said, "Father, all this man's sin, all his mistakes, every evil action, word and thought—all of his shortcomings—put them all down against Me; Daniel Curry stood for me down on the earth; I'll stand for him up here."

"Whosoever therefore shall confess me before men, him will I confess also before my Father which is in heaven. But whosoever shall deny me before men, him will I also deny before my Father which is in heaven" (Matt. 10:32, 33).

May you stand for Jesus Christ here, confess Him and love Him so that He will stand for you in Heaven and confess you and reward you for faithfully serving Him.

THE JUDGMENT SEAT OF CHRIST

Early in my Christian life, I received a book that has meant a great deal to me. I learned from this book, *The Judgment Seat of Christ* by Dr. L. Sale-Harrison, the importance of living "with eternity's values in view." I have since then read everything I can find on this profoundly important subject, of which Dr. John. F. Walvoord said, "There is no more practical prophetic truth than this simple pointed doctrine of the judgment seat of Christ."[1]

Dr. W. Myrddin Lewis, prophetic scholar of England, wrote of this judgment in these words: "Here too is a thought that *should* be the greatest inducement to holy living, greater than any other single thing."[2]

WHAT?

The phrase "the Judgment Seat of Christ" appears only twice in the Bible, but it is referred to many times. The first direct use of the phrase is found in Romans 14:10: "But why dost thou judge thy brother? or why dost thou set at nought thy brother? for we shall all stand before *the judgment seat of Christ*" (italics added). The second and only other use of this wording is in 2 Corinthians 5:10: "For we must all appear before *the judgment seat of Christ;* that every one may receive the things done in his body, according to that he hath done, whether it be good or bad" (italics added). In these two passages, God is speaking of Christians, who *must* all stand or appear before this judgment. The "we" in 2 Corinthians 5:10 is used twenty-six times in this chapter and always refers to believers in Christ.

The words "judgment seat" are a translation of the Greek word *bema*, which is a raised platform. In Paul's day, outside the city of Corinth stood a large Olympic stadium containing a raised platform on which the judge sat and watched the contestants. When the contests were finished, the contestants assembled before the Bema Seat to receive their rewards. The Bible speaks of the Christian life as a race (1 Cor. 9:24; Heb. 12:1). The judge, the Lord Jesus Christ, is watching every Christian; and when the race is finished and the Lord Jesus returns for His own, each Christian will receive that which he has done in the body (1 Cor. 4:5; 2 Cor. 5:10).

This is not a judgment of the unsaved. Only Christians will be at this judgment. Christ will judge the works done from the time an individual became a Christian.

WHEN?

Paul wrote in 1 Corinthians 4:5: "Therefore judge nothing before the time, *until the Lord come*, who both will bring to light the hidden things of darkness, and will make manifest the counsels of the hearts: *and then* shall every man have praise of God" (italics added). Here we are told that the hidden things of darkness will be brought to light and that the counsels of the hearts will be made manifest (or exposed) when the Lord comes. Paul also instructed us: "Henceforth there is laid up for me a crown of righteousness, which the Lord, the righteous judge, shall give me at that day: and not to me only, but unto all them also that love his appearing" (2 Tim. 4:8). The crowns will be given to faithful Christians "at that day," the day of "his appearing." Jesus also told us when He would judge the Christians and reward those who were faithful to Him: "And, behold, I come quickly; and my reward is with me, to give every man according as his work shall be" (Rev. 22:12).

Dr. Isaac M. Haldeman, great prophetic preacher of some years ago, wrote: "According to the Word of God, the testimony of the Son of God and the corroborative and unbroken testimony of the apostles, there is not the thickness of tissue paper between us who are Christians and the Judgment Seat of Christ."[3]

In the light of the soon return of our Lord Jesus Christ and our appearing before Him to give an account of our Christian lives, these words of Dr. W. Myrddin Lewis should alert us:

> We see every major prophecy of God's word regarding our Lord's return fulfilled, including the great prophecy in Ezekiel 37, where God through the mouth of His servant foretold the uniting of the Jewish people into one nation, brought back from across the seven seas, and re-established in Palestine as a sovereign nation. With that now history, and with no other prophecy to be fulfilled that could possibly delay His coming, what manner of persons ought we to be, in the light of this truth that any minute now we shall be snatched from off this sinful, evil and wicked earth to stand in His presence before His Judgment Seat?[4]

WHY?

I wish to make it unquestionably clear that this judgment is only for Christians, not for the unsaved. Dr. J. Dwight Pentecost wrote of this in these words:

> The word translated "appear" in 2 Corinthians 5:10 might better be rendered "to be made manifest," so that the verse reads, "For it is necessary for all of us to be made manifest." This suggests that the purpose of the bema is to make a public manifestation, demonstration or revelation of the essential character and motives of the individual. Plummer's remark: "We shall not be judged *en masse*, or in classes, but one by one, in accordance with individual merit," substantiates the fact that this is an individual judgment of each believer before the Lord.[5]

In 2 Corinthians 5:10, Paul gave the reason for our appearing before the Judgment Seat of Christ: "That every one may receive the things done in his body, according to that he hath done, whether it be good or bad."

In 1 Corinthians 3:10–15, God spoke of the Judgment Seat:

> According to the grace of God which is given unto me, as a wise masterbuilder, I have laid the foundation, and another buildeth thereon. But let every man take heed how he buildeth thereupon. For

other foundation can no man lay than that is laid, which is Jesus Christ. Now if any man build upon this foundation gold, silver, precious stones, wood, hay, stubble; Every man's work shall be made manifest: for the day shall declare it, because it shall be revealed by fire; and the fire shall try every man's work of what sort it is. If any man's work abide which he hath built thereupon, he shall receive a reward. If any man's work shall be burned, he shall suffer loss: but he himself shall be saved; yet so as by fire.

Here Paul says that only one foundation exists on which we should build our lives, and that is Jesus Christ. He also warned us in verse 10: "But let every man take heed how he buildeth thereupon." Then he speaks of the different kinds of materials a Christian can use in building: "gold, silver, precious stones, wood, hay, stubble." Note the distinct contrast in the materials: gold, silver, precious stones or wood, hay, stubble. The gold, silver and precious stones speak figuratively of that which is permanent, in contrast to that which is perishing, represented by the wood, hay and stubble. They contrast worthiness to worthlessness, quality to quantity, the Spirit to the flesh, living for eternity to living only for time, that which is done in the will of God to that which is done in the will of man, and that which is done for the glory of God to that which is done for the glory of man.

In verse 13 we are told that our works will be tried or tested by fire. Fire is a symbol of deity: "For the LORD thy God is a consuming fire, even a jealous God" (Deut. 4:24); "For our God is a consuming fire" (Heb. 12:29). Revelation 1:14 says of Jesus Christ, "His eyes were as a flame of fire." Jeremiah 23:29 speaks of the Word of God as fire: "Is not my word like as a fire? saith the LORD." The Holy Spirit of God is referred to as "the spirit of burning" in Isaiah 4:4. Putting these three thoughts together, we conclude: When a holy God tests our works and service, only that which has been done according to the Word of God and in the power of the Holy Spirit will be approved and rewarded.

REWARDS

The Christian who has lived in the Spirit and according to the Word of God will be rewarded—"he shall receive a reward" (1 Cor.

3:14). Scripture speaks of five crowns that will be given to faithful Christians:
1. the Incorruptible Crown (1 Cor. 9:25–27), for running the Christian race well and keeping his body under subjection;
2. the Crown of Rejoicing (1 Thess. 2:19, 20), for winning souls;
3. the Crown of Righteousness (2 Tim. 4:8), for loving the appearing of Jesus Christ;
4. the Crown of Life (James 1:12; Rev. 2:10), for enduring trials and loving the Lord in spite of the trials, even to the point of death;
5. the Crown of Glory (1 Pet. 5:1–4), for being a faithful pastor and feeding the flock of God willingly and with a ready mind.

In Revelation 4:10 and 11, we read of the time when the twenty-four elders cast their crowns before the throne to give glory and honor and power to the Lord. Dr. E. Schuyler English said, "They represent, unless I am badly mistaken, the raptured church after her receipt of the awards given out at the *bēma* of Christ."[6] Dr. Pentecost commented:

> In Revelation 4:10, where the elders are seen to be casting their crowns before the throne in an act of worship and adoration, it is made clear that the crowns will not be for the eternal glory of the recipient, but for the glory of the Giver. Since these crowns are not viewed as a permanent possession, the question of the nature of the rewards themselves arises. From the Scriptures it is learned that the believer was redeemed in order that he might bring glory to God (1 Cor. 6:20). This becomes his eternal destiny. The act of placing the material sign of a reward at the feet of the One who sits on the throne (Rev. 4:10) is one act in that glorification. But the believer will not then have completed his destiny to glorify God. This will continue throughout eternity. The greater the reward, the greater the bestowed capacity to bring glory to God. Thus in the exercise of the reward of the believer, it will be Christ and not the believer that is glorified by the reward.[7]

When Queen Victoria listened to the "Hallelujah Chorus" in the Albert Hall in London, she instantly rose to her feet. When someone asked her why she had done so, she replied: "My Lord is coming one day. I would love for Him to come now so that I could, as Queen of Britain and Empress of India, take my crowns and lay them at His feet." She believed in Jesus Christ as her personal Savior and Lord and eagerly waited for Him to return. Dr. F. E. Marsh told an interesting story about rewards:

> It is said that Ivan, of Russia, used sometimes to disguise himself, and go out among his people to find out their true character. One night he went, dressed as a beggar, into the suburbs of Moscow, and asked for a night's lodging, but he was refused admittance at every house, until at last, his heart sank with discouragement to think of the selfishness of his people. At length, however, he knocked at a door where he was gladly admitted. The poor man invited him in, offered him a crust of bread, a cup of water, and a bed of straw, and then said, "I am sorry I cannot do more for you, but my wife is ill, a babe has just been given her, and my attention is needed for them." The Emperor lay down and slept the sleep of a contented mind. He had found a true heart. In the morning he took his leave with many thanks.
>
> The poor man forgot all about it, until a few days later, the royal chariot drove up to the door, and attended by his retinue, the Emperor stopped at his humble abode.
>
> The poor man was alarmed, and throwing himself at the Emperor's feet, asked, "What have I done?"
>
> Ivan lifted him up, and taking him by both his hands, said, "Done! You've done nothing but entertain your Emperor. It was I who lay upon that bed of straw, it was I who received your humble but hearty hospitality, and now I have come to reward you. You received me in disguise, but now I come in my true character to recompense your love. Bring hither your new-born babe." And as he brought him, he said, "You shall call him after me, and when he is old enough, I will educate him and give him a place in my court and service." Giving him a bag of gold, he said, "Use this for your wife, and if ever you have need of anything, don't forget to call upon the poor tramp that slept the other night in the corner."

Something similar will happen when our Lord returns. For every cup of water given in His name, for every kindly word spoken for His sake, for every meal given out of love to Him, for every encouragement given to others, for every self-denying act to our brethren, there will be recognition and recompense from our Lord Jesus Christ.[8]

Dr. Marsh concluded his chapter entitled "The Worker's Rewards" with these encouraging words:

> Let us remember that not a single action done out of love to Christ shall miss His commendation and reward in the day of His reckoning. Everything done for "His name's sake" is recorded for our reward. He records the ardent faith of a clinging soul [Matthew 15:28]; the generous heart which gives its all, although it be but two mites [Luke 21:2–4]; the true confession of Himself is music in His ears, and calls forth His approbation [Matthew 16:17]; He appreciates the breaking of the costly box of ointment over His person, and makes a lasting memorial of it [Matthew 26:13]; He commends the earnest desire of David to build Him a temple, and puts the building down to His account, although he never placed a stone in it [2 Samuel 7:2–17; 1 Chronicles 28:2]; He is careful to give as much reward to the prophet's host, as He gives to the prophet himself [Matthew 10:41], and the cup of water given to one of His own is accepted as done to Himself [Mark 9:41].[9]

Jesus said, "Behold, I come quickly: hold that fast which thou hast, that no man take thy crown" (Rev. 3:11). We are encouraged in 2 John 8, "Look to yourselves, that we lose not those things which we have wrought, but that we receive a full reward."

Charles C. Luther has written words that should stir our hearts:

> Must I go, and empty-handed, Thus my dear Redeemer meet?
> Not one day of service give Him, Lay no trophy at His feet?
> Not at death I shrink nor falter, For my Savior saves me now;
> But to meet Him empty-handed, Thought of that now clouds my brow.
> O the years in sinning wasted! Could I but recall them now,

I would give them to my Savior—To His will I'd gladly bow.
O ye saints, arouse, be earnest, Up and work while yet 'tis day;
Ere the night of death o'ertake thee, Strive for souls while still you
    may.
Must I go, and empty-handed? Must I meet my Savior so?
Not one soul with which to greet Him—Must I empty-handed go?

LOSS

"If any man's work shall be burned, he shall suffer loss: but he himself shall be saved; yet so as by fire" (1 Cor. 3:15). Those works done by a Christian—which were not done according to the Word of God, which were not done in the power of the Holy Spirit but in the flesh, which were not done because of love for the Lord but for love of self, which were not done for the glory of God but to glorify man—will be burned up as "wood, hay, stubble," and the unfaithful Christian will suffer loss. This does not mean the loss of the soul, because the verse goes on to say, "But he himself shall be saved; yet so as by fire." This has the thought of a man asleep in his house while his house catches fire. Someone comes along, sees the fire, rushes in, drags the man out through the fire and takes him to safety. The house and everything in it is burned to the ground, but the man is saved "yet only as in passing through fire" (1 Cor. 3:15, Berkeley).

Dr. Lehman Strauss commented on the loss:

> We hear much preaching to Christians about the rewards they will get in heaven, but we hear very little preaching about those Christians who will "suffer loss." Of course, the latter subject is less popular. But my Christian friend, none of us can afford to be careless and indifferent, because it will make a big difference in the end. I do not know all that is meant by the words "suffer loss," but we may be certain they do not mean that we will enjoy our losses. What shame and regrets are suggested in this prospect![10]

Nor do I know all that is meant by the words "suffer loss," but in the rest of this chapter I want to share with you what I have found in my studies. I realize that all Christians do not share these views, but I pray that every Christian who reads this will be like the

Bereans, of whom it was said, "They received the word with all readiness of mind, and searched the scriptures daily, whether those things were so" (Acts 17:11). I will quote quite extensively from a number of men of God of the past and present who have written concerning the Judgment Seat of Christ.

Dr. Keith L. Brooks:

> Some seem to think that if we are Christians, God is not going to bring up anything done in this life. It is all "under the blood." Put everything on Jesus and live any way you please. Surely that cannot be right.
>
> There has undoubtedly been too much emphasis on the "rewards for works" side of the teaching concerning the Judgment Seat of Christ (Rom. 14:10; II Cor. 5:10). It is of primary importance to understand that, while *salvation* is free through the grace of God (John 4:10; Rom. 6:23; Rev. 22:17, etc.) if we have *rewards*, it will be because we have built up enduring works on the Foundation of Jesus Christ as our personal Saviour (I Cor. 3:11–15; 9:24; Luke 19:17; Matt. 10:24, etc.).
>
> Many Christians will see much of their "church work" go up as a puff of smoke—"wood, hay and stubble"—because it had nothing to do with the salvation of souls or edification of the saints, and was therefore without enduring quality. Even that could make one most uncomfortable standing before Christ's Judgment Seat.
>
> But, there is another side, for the word "Bema" rendered "Judgment Seat," signifies a place where judgment is rendered and that judgment will have to do not only with our works, but our witness, our stewardship, our LIVING. The Christian's DOING will pass in review—will be exposed. All those matters never confessed and made right with man and God, will come up as on a great screen and it is quite possible that within a brief space of time, one might experience pangs of shame equal to years of mortal sorrows.
>
> First John 2:28 says expressly that some will (lit.) "shrink in shame from Him." At His coming is the time and place where stubborn

Christians will be caught up with for all those things never made right. It would appear that even those spirits coming with Him from the heavenly side after long waiting the day of the Judgment Seat, will be capable of having such matters drawn from their memories, for the judgment of all believers is represented as taking place at the same time—when He comes. Bear in mind that the spirits in heaven will not until that time receive their completed condition nor could their works until then be summed up.)

Dr. Graham Scroggie, writing to a friend, once said: "I would rather go through the Great Tribulation than endure what I believe some Christians will go through at the Judgment Seat of Christ."(In the white light of His glory, who can say what his capacity for a sense of mortification may be when faced with a moving picture of wrongs neither confessed nor straightened out?) . .

("He that doeth wrong shall receive for the wrong he hath done *and there is no respect of persons*" (Col. 3:25). Christ will "bring to light the hidden things and will make manifest the counsels of the hearts" (I Cor. 4:5).) We shall receive according to what we have done, *"Whether it be good or bad"* (II Cor. 5:10).

(Teachers of the Word are responsible to warn believers that while God may send them chastening in this life for many of their misdeeds (I Cor. 11:31, 32; Col. 3:25; Heb. 12:7–9) there will still be a day of reckoning for matters left unadjusted at the time they are called out of this world.[11])

Dr. M. R. DeHaan:

Before they can reign in righteousness with Him, a lot of things which are all wrong among believers now will have to be made right, first. If we do not make them right now, they will be made right at the judgment seat of Christ, and it will not be a pleasant experience for many to see their works burned up and they themselves saved so as by fire, and then consigned to a lower place in the Kingdom with loss of rewards and with many sad regrets.

If Jesus were to return today, I fear that He would find many, many believers quite unprepared for His coming. Those who are living in unconfessed sin and bitterness and pride; Christians who are carnal, selfish and worldly; Christians who are wasting their talents, opportunities, time and privileges. Do not imagine for a moment that these things will all be passed over in grace and forgotten when Jesus comes. Before we can reign with Him, we must be perfectly, spotlessly clean, and if we refuse it now, it will be done at the Judgment Seat of Christ. This is the purpose for this judgment of believers.[2]

Dr. Theodore H. Epp:

At the Judgment Seat of Christ, difficulties and inequalities among the saints will be ironed out. We have so many of these in our present day. All the injustices and misunderstandings of God's people among themselves will then be settled. Those of the saints who were humble, and who endured meekly and unresistingly accusation and malicious gossip for Christ's sake, even from fellow believers, will be manifested in their true light. They will then be vindicated in the eyes of all, and cleared of all false charges.

We must not overlook the fact that those who in their pride have done and said wrong things, unless they have confessed these things to God and renounced them, will face the consequences of such conduct at the Judgment Seat of Christ by losing rewards.[3]

Dr. Lehman Strauss:

The judgment seat of Christ seems a necessity to the writer. Think of the believers, all members of the body of Christ, who are divided because of differences. In organizations, in churches, and in families I have seen Christians who are not on speaking terms. People who were at one time very close and intimate friends are now separated, and a bitter feeling exists between them. Each blames the separation on the other, and they continue on, trying to serve the Lord, but their difference has not been adjusted. Now if our Lord returns before there is a reconciliation of such Christians here on earth, it is necessary that they get right with each other somewhere, for certainly they cannot continue on forever in holding hatred and animosity in their hearts. Heaven knows no such actions. Hatred and unforgiveness is sin. Yet there is no sin in Heaven. Hence the necessity of the judgment seat of Christ.)[4]

Dr. Emery H. Bancroft:

(There will be a vast amount of healthy work transacted at the judgment seat of Christ. . . . The mistakes of time will there be rectified; wrong judgments reversed, misunderstandings corrected; ungenerous attempts to impute falsehood or evil where such do not exist, exposed; and, in short, persons, ways, words, motives and acts shall then appear in their true light and character. It will be a clearing up moment. . . . Every difficulty and question between believers and God, and between brother and brother shall then be righteously adjusted.)[5]

Dr. Isaac Haldeman:

Each Christian must give an account to Him. You cannot give an account for me. I cannot give an account for you. You must give an account for yourself. I must give an account for myself. We will have to make our speech to Him, give a narrative of our lives as Christians. We shall have to give a reason for what we did and what we did not do. We shall have to tell Him why we neglected His Holy Word, the exercise of prayer, the house of God; and why again and again we refused to meet the responsibility of the profession we made or the service into which He called us. Everything will come out in that all-searching light.

. . . Confessed sins will not appear at the Judgment Seat of Christ. Unconfessed sins will be revealed and will weigh the scales of judgment in relation to our work and service. . . .

(At this Judgment Seat all things will be adjusted by the Lord. All things will be righted and regulated)[16]

Dr. Donald G. Barnhouse:

All our dealings with fellow Christians must be brought out at the return of the Lord Jesus Christ. The innuendo, slander, backbiting, envy, jealousy, gossiping and lying among Christians is a first-class scandal. . . .

My mind has been very much occupied with thoughts that have grown out of my studies concerning our appearance before the judgment seat of God in Christ. Can we remain careless when we realize that all our deeds will be reviewed there? Unsettled accounts will be fully opened and settled. What we have done as Christians will face us there. . . .

The question is now asked: But if we confess our sins, do we not find forgiveness? Certainly. But after the sinner has found mercy, and after the saint has found forgiveness, several things remain to be dealt with. Do we think for one moment that the terrible words "that shall he also reap" [Galatians 6:7] apply to this life alone? Shall not much of the reaping be done beyond the grave?

. . . Can we think for one moment that death is sufficient to wipe out the neglected duties, the lost opportunities, and the wasted times of this life?

. . . We may be sure that the consequences of our character will survive the grave and that we shall face those consequences at the judgment seat of Christ.[17]

Dr. W. H. Griffith Thomas:

. . . While a genuine Christian who becomes a backslider will not be judicially condemned forever, there *will* be a very serious measure of personal and *practical condemnation* when such an one stands before the judgment seat of Christ to be dealt with according to works since conversion.[18]

Dr. W. Myrddin Lewis:

In 1 John 2:28 we read: "And now, little children, abide in him; that, when He shall appear, we may have confidence, and not be ashamed before Him at His coming." Now, the words "not be ashamed" clearly suggest that the Judgment Seat of Christ will be a place where many of His people will be ashamed. They also suggest that it will be a place where many tears of shame will be shed by countless numbers of His people, who in their pilgrimage on earth, failed in their stewardship and thus were made unworthy of the crown which He had set aside for them the day that they were saved.) . . .

. . . It may be well if we again, in the light of His immediate appearing, examine ourselves so that no known sin or wrong is left unconfessed, for if we neglect this God-given, merciful exercise and arrive at the Judgment Seat with unconfessed wrongs and sins, then bitter indeed will be our tears as we stand before Him in the presence of all heaven and all His people. . . .[19]

Evangelist John Linton:

Scripture declares that God is keeping a record of the sinner's thoughts, words and deeds. Before an assembled universe at the great white throne in heaven, each man's record will be read out. When the unsaved man stands before God to have his record unfolded, will there be any tears shed there in Heaven? What think ye?

But God is also keeping a record of certain sins of the saints. This record includes all unconfessed sin due to an unrepentant heart; all unforgiven sin due to an unforgiving spirit; and all unfaithful service due to an unsurrendered life. A backsliding Christian who dies in his unfaithfulness will face his record at the judgment seat of Christ. A Christian who had wronged his brother and has never repented of his sin before God and man, will have that unconfessed and unforgiven sin to face at the judgment seat of Christ. Question: When the record of his wrongdoing is read out before the whole assembled Church, will there be any tears of shame and regret shed there in Heaven? What think ye?

When the unfaithful Christian reads in the light of eternity the story of his unfaithfulness; when he realizes that the cause of Christ has sorely suffered by his indifference and neglect; when he sees that through him souls have been lost to hell who could have been won for heaven; when he fails to hear the "Well done" given to him that is given to the faithful servants, will that Christian be utterly unmoved by the revelation of his failure? No sorrow over a lost reward? No regret over despised opportunities? No tears of shame in Heaven? What think ye?

Here is a Christian man who has grievously wronged his brother. He never repents of that sin before God or man. He makes a general confession of what he calls "all my sins," but he never drags this particular sin out of its hiding place. He lives and dies unrepentant with that sin unconfessed. What will happen when that man stands before the judgment seat of Christ? The brother he wronged is standing there beside him. What will God do about that? Why, you say, that man will be changed in a moment into the likeness of Christ. He will know nothing but joy in Heaven. Salvation is by grace and all our sins are under the blood of Christ. God will welcome that man into heaven and never mention his sin, whether confessed or unconfessed. My friend, to make that statement is to construe the grace of God as license; is to impugn the holiness of God; is to ignore the fact of human responsibility and to deny the plainest teaching of the Bible. Jesus said, "If thou bring thy gift to the altar, and there rememberest that thy brother hath ought against thee: leave there thy gift before the altar and go thy way: first be reconciled to thy brother, and then come and offer thy gift." If that be required at the altar down here, will it not be required at the altar up yonder? Is the command "first be reconciled" true on earth, but not true once we get to heaven?

Yes, Christians will be brought face to face at the judgment seat with every alienated brother, with every unredressed wrong, with every unconfessed sin, with all unfaithful service.[20]

Alexander Patterson as quoted by John Linton:

There is a searching process here which will be terrible to work done from wrong motives, or works left undone. The judgment of Christ is of persons as well as their works. "Saved as by fire" intimates a searching personal examination. Every secret thing not repented of and confessed, will be exposed, to the shame and mortification of the doer. Paul writes of issues to come up in this judgment: "Therefore judge nothing before the time, until the Lord come, who both will bring to light the hidden things of darkness, and will make manifest the counsels of the hearts: and then shall every man have praise of God.' All wrong estimates of men will be set right and the result will be as Christ has said, "many that are first will be last, and the last will be first." All idle words, as Christ said, will be accounted for at the day of this judgment. All unsettled quarrels will be brought to account.[21]

Dr. H. H. Savage:

God's judgment seat is not anything to look forward to with anticipation if there is sin in your heart. It is a fearful thing for God's own children to face Him when He says, "Why weren't you doing what you ought to have done? Why weren't you living as you should have lived? Why weren't you as true to Me as you should have been? Why weren't you?" For we shall all stand before the judgment seat of Christ.

. . . Those at the judgment seat of Christ are going to have to confess before Him the things that still need to be confessed. Those who are critics, those who are faultfinders, those who are character assassins, those who are doing everything they can to bring about schisms and difficulties in the church will have to report to Him. They have to confess to Him what sort of influence they have had on earth.[22]

Dr. L. Sale-Harrison:

The seriousness of a Christian's life of failure is clearly outlined in many portions of God's Word, for the life lived outside God's will suffers a dual loss. It has a serious effect on his earthly life in loss of power, joy and communion with God; but the loss revealed at the Judgment Seat of Christ is even more tragic. . . .

Sin must be judged. God cannot condone it. If He does, then He is approving of unrighteousness. This He cannot do. God's grace so marvelously manifested to a Christian cannot be an excuse for sin. If we are not willing to judge ourselves after the Holy Spirit convicts us, then it must be judged at the Judgment Seat of Christ. It must be judged either here, or there; but it must be judged. . . .

Read again 1 John 1:9: "If we confess our sins, he is faithful and just to forgive us our sins, and to cleanse us from all unrighteousness." Therefore if we do not confess our sins, that unrighteousness—which has not been cleansed—must be manifested (exposed) at the Judgment Seat of Christ. . . .

May we be led by the Spirit of God to examine ourselves and seek the removal of all things which mar fellowship with the Lord; for some do not realize how serious a sin it is to trifle with our opportunities, and to walk out of fellowship with Him.[23]

John R. Rice:

But return again to the Scripture, II Corinthians 5:9–11. Saved people are to receive according to things done in the body, "whether it be good or bad." Those who have done good will have joy and praise from Christ. Do you think those who are reproved for having done bad will not be sad? There, no doubt, will flow some tears!

In fact, to face Christ at that time will be a terror to those who have failed to do His bidding after they were saved. I say "terror"—that is exactly what Paul wrote of that time, by inspiration of God: "Knowing therefore the terror of the Lord," Paul says after describing that judgment of Christians, "we persuade men." I once thought that verse was speaking of the terror with which lost men will face Christ, but it is not so. Knowing the terror that will fall on saved people, saints in Heaven after the rapture who face Christ after a wasted life, Paul went about persuading other Christians to do as he did, laboring that he might be acceptable to Christ when he should stand before the Saviour! In Heaven it will be terrible to face Christ who saved you and keeps you, in your shame over your wasted life! Tears in Heaven!

Paul urged Timothy to be "a workman that needeth not to be ashamed" (II Tim. 2:15), and doubtless spoke of this same time when saints in Heaven will be ashamed and sad as they face Jesus their Saviour. I am not speaking of punishment now, but of tears, of shame and sadness. Surely there will be tears in Heaven over our failure and wasted opportunities.[24]

Dr. S. Franklin Logsdon:

It is a solemn engagement indeed to project our thoughts toward this day when, on bended knees before the fiery eyes of Omniscience, we face the record. Yet the prevailing thought, if any consideration at all is given to it, is that Christ will be a mild-mannered examiner of deeds, and the careless believer continues in his self-centeredness, singing all the while, "That will be glory for me. . . ."

We find a number of these pointed warnings regarding the Judgment Seat of Christ, couched in terse, incisive language. They are warnings which, admittedly, we have not taken very seriously. We either ignore them completely or relegate them to other people or transfer their application to another dispensation. Let us briefly allude to three.

The Vengeance of the Lord. "The Lord shall judge his people" (Heb. 10:30, last line). This statement is concise and clear. There can be nothing ambiguous about it. The term "my people" rules out the unbeliever and the Great White Throne judgment. Its position in the context rules out the Old Testament Jewish saints, for the statement stands in contradistinction to Moses' law in verse 28. The verb is of emphatic future tense, and what other judgment for New Testament believers could be in view if not the Judgment Seat of Christ? It speaks of those who are "sanctified" but who have "done despite to the Spirit of grace." There is to be a time of reckoning for this type of unspiritual behavior.

Now, the disturbing feature of this whole revelation is the immediate statement that "It is a fearful thing to fall into the hands of the living God" (Heb. 10:31). We make no attempt to interpret this, but we do remind the reader with much solemnity that, whatever its sobering content, it is directly connected to the information that "the Lord shall judge his [own] people."

The Terror of the Lord. In seeking to register with the people the seriousness of the inevitable confrontation with Christ at the *bema,* Paul immediately added this, "Knowing therefore the terror of the Lord, we persuade men" (II Cor. 5:11). Again, we will attempt no explanation, for neither did the apostle. Anticipating the reactions to this outburst of concern, he said, "For if we are beside ourselves (mad, as some would say), it is for God and concerns Him; if we are in our right mind, it is for your benefit" (II Cor. 5:13, *Amplified*).

An Appropriate Retribution. The Spirit of God has gone to great pains to detail character and conduct for believers, making clear their responsibilities both to God and to man. According to Hebrews 2:1, there is a fearful tendency toward flagrant carelessness, letting such practical truths slip by. The next verse clearly warns that, for every violation and disobedience, there will be an appropriate penalty. How can it be otherwise since God is just? And, further, "How shall we escape (appropriate retribution) if we neglect and refuse to pay attention to such great salvation?" (Heb. 2:3, *Amplified*).[25]

Dr. F. E. Marsh:

. . . The light of the Lord's presence will illuminate our life, and reveal every secret of our heart; for the counsels of the heart will be revealed, and the hidden things will be seen in the light. What a revelation it will be! Ambitions, not of the Lord, will be seen. Black bitterness against others will be detected. Covetousness of the heart will be unmasked. Deviations from the truth will be discovered. Envyings of others will be revealed. Fault-finding with our brethren will be discerned. Grumblings and murmurings will be disclosed. Heart backslidings and secret faults will be made known. Indulgings of the flesh and selfishness will be unearthed. Judging of others wrongfully will be unfolded. Love of money, ease, and the world will be descried. Mixed motives in work for Christ will be ferreted out. Opportunities lost for doing good and confessing Christ will be shown up. Perverseness of heart, and pleasures not of God will be apparent. Quarrellings, backbiting, anger, and malice will be seen.

Rebelliousness and repinings under God's chastening hand will be distinguished. Selfishness, slanderings, and self-will will be observed. Tremblings before the world will be palpable. Uncleanness of heart will be recognized. Willfulness and wanderings will be visible. Yearnings for the flesh pots of Egypt will be evident; and zealousness to be had in honour of men will be made plain.[26]

Dr. Robert T. Ketcham:

The question of what happens to the believer whose works are all burned up has been a vexing one. Does he go into the millennial reign as a sort of "silent partner"? Since he has no crown of reward, what position *does* he hold in the reign?

Scripture says the reigning is contingent upon the suffering. Second Timothy 2:12: "If we suffer, we shall also reign with him: if we deny him, he also will deny us." What about the believer who has never really "suffered" with Christ? What is his status in the reign? . . .

. . . I do not think the worldly believer will share in the millennial reign.[27]

Then Dr. Ketcham, in his sermon "The Carnal Christian at the Judgment Seat of Christ," convincingly told why he believed the Scriptures teach that those who do not suffer with Christ, those who do not surrender to Christ and serve Him faithfully, will not reign with Him during the Millennium. He continued:

. . . Let us put it into an understandable picture. The millennial reign is now on. Day after day King Emmanuel sends His co-reigning bride to the ends of His universe to carry out His biddings. When all the assignments are made for the day, I find myself sitting alone and unassigned. I ask the Lord what *I* am to do in His kingdom today. He replies, "Nothing." I cry out, "Why, Lord, am I not allowed to do something for You today?" He will reply, "Because you were content to do nothing for Me before you arrived here!" Believe me, dear reader, *that* would be "outer darkness" enough for me! Just to see others of my friends and fellow Christians with whom I associated down here going out day after day in responsible co-reigning with my Lord and I am denied that privilege because I took the easy way here will be enough to cause me to weep and sorrow. Just to see others going here and there *for* Him and *with* Him and I must remain behind would be "outer darkness" enough! I want none of it. . . .

The general attitudes concerning the matters discussed in this chapter are: *First:* There will be rewards for faithfulness in various lines of Christian living. *Second:* The believer *does* sin, and, as a consequence, receives chastisement, but it is confined to this life only. *Third:* Some believers will have *no* reward at the Judgment Seat of Christ, but because *chastisement* ends with *this* life, there will be none there.

The difference between this common conception and the view set forth in this chapter is simply this: The *principle* of chastisement remains the same; the difference is in the *extent* to which it is to be carried. One halts the process at the Judgment Seat of Christ; the other allows its continuance for those who did not submit to its benefactions here. I have searched in vain for a single Scripture to prove the discontinuance of this principle at the Lord's return. On the other hand a great mass of Scripture, the *most* of which I have not mentioned here, seems to indicate the awful and soul-searching truth that there is such a thing as corrective discipline when we see Him face to face.

We have been surprised to discover that many teachers have had a conviction that this was the teaching of Scripture, such men as Lange, Dean Alford, Stanley, Goebel, and Govett. And when we read the following from the pen of C. G. Trumbull, editor of *The Sunday School Times*, are we not led to believe he had some convictions along this line? Writing of the parable of the talents, he said: "If the servant (who is cast into outer darkness) is *not* a believer, but a mere professor, then we have in this parable nothing to represent the Christian who fails in faithfulness." [28]

Dr. Herbert Lockyer, in an excellent article, "The Advent and Youth," agreed that believers must experience the Judgment Seat of Christ before they are qualified to serve Him in the Kingdom. He saw as a prime function of the Bema Seat the restoration of broken or damaged fellowship among believers. "As the judgment seat of Christ is not a criminal court, but a court of inquiry, it is logical to assume that the Lord and His own are to be alone as all disputes are settled, and all relationships harmonized." [29] In this light, Dr. Lockyer urges the settling of differences now, rather than waiting to experience the shame of adjusting them in front of Christ.

As one of the many Bible teachers who teach that our place and position in the coming world will be decided at the Judgment Seat, Dr. Lockyer observed, "What the great majority of Christians lose sight of is the fact that they are presently developing themselves for future positions in Christ's coming kingdom."[30] He urges greater loyalty to the Lord and the Word and greater service so that we may have "an abundant entrance" into the Lord's presence.

Evangelist Kenneth F. Dodson:

> The words, "suffer loss" have a far greater significance than many believers realize. Both the Lord Jesus and the Apostle Paul point out that the greatest reward for the victorious, overcoming child of God will be the privilege of sitting upon the throne with the Lord Jesus and reigning with Him over this earth for a thousand years. The Lord Jesus said, "To him that overcometh will I grant to sit with me in my throne" (Rev. 3:21a). (See also Rev. 20:4.) Paul said, "If we suffer, we shall also reign as kings together with him: if we deny him, he also will deny us [the privilege of reigning with him]" (II Tim. 2:12—[a] literal [translation of the] Greek).

> Actually, for the Christian, the judgment seat of Christ is God's gateway into the Millennial Kingdom of the Lord Jesus Christ. It is there that every Christian's position in the thousand year reign will be determined on the basis of God's just evaluation of the Christian's life in this sinful world. According to Paul's peerless philosophy of life expressed in Romans 8:28, 29, everything in the Christian's daily life is designed of God to make the Christian worthy of reigning with the Lord Jesus, so that "He may be the first-born among many brethren," in His glorious kingdom. Did not the Lord Jesus, Himself, say that some would reign with Him over ten cities and some would be "unprofitable servants," stripped of every reward? (Luke 19:11–26).

> So, the Christian who is not willing to take his stand for Christ "in this wicked and adulterous generation," and accept the persecution

which is bound to come (II Tim. 3:12), will really "suffer loss" for a thousand years. He will see some other Christian who was willing to be either a "living martyr" (Rom. 12:1, 2) or a "dying martyr" (Rev. 20:4) sitting with the Lord Jesus in the place of honor which might have been his. He will see what a fool he was for spending his time and energy for the gadgets and material baubles of a twentieth century civilization instead of "seeking first the Kingdom of God and His righteousness" (Matt. 6:33). He will not lose his salvation, but he will have a "so-as-by-fire entrance" instead of an "abundant entrance into the everlasting kingdom of our Lord and Saviour, Jesus Christ" (II Peter 1:11).

Since the "kings" of the millennial earth bring their "honor and glory" into the heavenly city on "the earth" (Rev. 21:24) the Christian's foolish preoccupation with "the things which are seen" may cost him the loss of the greatest possible reward for all eternity—the privilege of reigning with the Lord Jesus Christ over "the principalities and powers" of all interstellar space "unto the ages of the ages." How many of God's born-again children are living realistically in the light of the eternal consequences of every thought, word and deed of their lives?

. . . Paul makes it very clear that there will be real judgment of Christians' unconfessed, unforsaken sins at the judgment seat of Christ. To the Colossian Christians he wrote, "Whatsoever ye do, do it heartily, as to the Lord, and not unto men; knowing that of the Lord ye shall receive the reward of the inheritance: for ye serve the Lord Christ. *But he that doeth wrong shall receive for the wrong which he hath done,* and there is no respect of persons" (Col. 3:23–25). To the Corinthians, he wrote, "For we walk by faith and not by sight. We are confident, I say, and willing to be away from home in the body, and to be at home with the Lord. Wherefore, we are ambitious, that whether at home or away from home, we may be well pleasing to Him. For we must all be exposed to view before the judgment seat of Christ; that every one may receive the things done in his body, according to that he hath done, whether it be good or evil. Knowing therefore the terror of the Lord, we persuade men" (II Cor. 5:7–11, in a literal translation of the Greek).

One very well-read Bible teacher in a large church was very much disturbed at the thought of a Christian facing actual judgment for sins at the judgment seat. She was quite sure that the passage in Colossians must refer to the judgment of Christians' unconfessed sins in this life, until she was asked where and when the victorious Christian will "receive the reward of the inheritance." This she had to admit would be received at the "judgment seat of Christ," so whatever he receives "for the wrong which he hath done," must also be at the bema-seat. Then, with regard to the passage in Corinthians, she said that the judgment was to be for "bad works" and not "sins." When she was asked to give a Scriptural distinction between "bad works" and "sins," she could not do so. Christians are constantly searching for some method of explaining away Paul's teaching concerning the judgment seat of Christ, but it cannot be done. "For we must be exposed to view before the judgment seat," and "there is no respect of persons." [31]

I have purposely quoted many Christian scholars. They have said that the loss at the Judgment Seat of Christ will be much greater than most of us have thought, not only at the time of the judgment itself but also extending through the millennial reign of Christ.

After speaking of the Judgment Seat of Christ in 2 Corinthians 5:10, Paul immediately said in the next verse: "Knowing therefore the terror [fear] of the Lord, we persuade men. . . ." I personally know the fear of God; therefore, I persuade men to trust the Lord, love Him, honor Him, obey Him and serve Him faithfully so that when we meet Him, we will not be "ashamed before him at his coming" (1 John 2:28). Instead we shall hear Him say to us: "Well done, thou good and faithful servant: thou hast been faithful over a few things, I will make thee ruler over many things: enter thou into the joy of thy lord" (Matt. 25:21).

Give heed to the words of the evangelist John Linton:

In conclusion, I urge every saved man and woman to get right with man. If there is a wrong to be righted, do it dear friend, while yet there is time. If there is a sin unconfessed, confess it this side of the judgment seat. Don't spoil that first interview with Christ by having to be rebuked for unfaithfulness. Give to the blessed Saviour the joy of saying to you, "Well done." Begin to live for that day and that world. If you have crossed over the line of separation turn back this very hour. Cut loose from the things that are sinful or even questionable. If your giving has not been worthy of Christ, start giving sacrificially and in real earnest before He comes or before death calls you hence. Start today laying up treasure in heaven. You will be there a long time to enjoy it. Give in the light of the judgment seat; forgive as you would be forgiven; live for eternity. And may He present you and me unblamable and unreprovable in His sight. . . .[32]

REWARDS AT THE JUDGMENT SEAT OF CHRIST

God is "a rewarder of them that diligently seek him" (Heb. 11:6). The time will come when "every man shall receive his own reward according to his own labour" (1 Cor. 3:8).

The New Scofield Reference Bible states:

> God, in the N. T. Scriptures, offers to the lost, salvation; and for the faithful service of the saved, He offers rewards. The passages are easily distinguished by remembering that salvation is invariably spoken of as a free gift (e.g. John 4:10; Rom. 6:23; Eph. 2:8–9), whereas rewards are earned by works (Mt. 10:42; Lk. 19:17; I Cor. 9:24–25; II Tim. 4:7–8; Rev. 2:10; 22:12). A further distinction is that salvation is a present possession (Lk. 7:50; John 3:36; 5:24; 6:47), whereas rewards are a future attainment, to be given at the rapture (Mt. 16:27; II Tim. 4:8; Rev. 22:12).[1]

Some of the rewards will be given in this life, others at the Judgment Seat of Christ.

WHAT GOD REWARDS

Keeping God's Word: "Moreover by them is thy servant warned: and in keeping of them there is great *reward*" (Ps. 19:11).

Sowing Righteousness: "To him that soweth righteousness shall be a sure *reward*" (Prov. 11:18).

Fearing the Commandment: "Whoso despiseth the word shall be destroyed: but he that feareth the commandment shall be *rewarded*" (Prov. 13:13).

Working Together: "Two are better than one; because they have a good *reward* for their labour" (Eccles. 4:9).

Suffering Persecution for Christ: "Blessed are ye, when men shall revile you, and persecute you, and shall say all manner of evil against you falsely, for my sake. Rejoice, and be exceeding glad: for great is your *reward* in heaven: for so persecuted they the prophets which were before you" (Matt. 5:11, 12).

Giving Alms Secretly: "That thine alms may be in secret: and thy Father which seeth in secret himself shall *reward* thee openly" (Matt. 6:4).

Praying Secretly: "But thou, when thou prayest, enter into thy closet, and when thou hast shut thy door, pray to thy Father which is in secret; and thy Father which seeth in secret shall *reward* thee openly" (Matt. 6:6).

Fasting Secretly: "That thou appear not unto men to fast, but unto thy Father which is in secret: and thy Father, which seeth in secret, shall *reward* thee openly" (Matt. 6:18).

Receiving a Prophet: "He that receiveth a prophet in the name of a prophet shall receive a prophet's *reward* . . ." (Matt. 10:41).

Receiving a Righteous Man: "And he that receiveth a righteous man in the name of a righteous man shall receive a righteous man's *reward*" (Matt. 10:41).

Giving a Cup of Cold Water: "And whosoever shall give to drink unto one of these little ones a cup of cold water only in the name of a disciple, verily I say unto you, he shall in no wise lose his *reward*" (Matt. 10:42).

Bearing Reproach for Christ: "Blessed are ye, when men shall hate you, and when they shall separate you from their company, and shall reproach you, and cast out your name as evil, for the Son of man's sake. Rejoice ye in that day, and leap for joy: for, behold, your *reward* is great in heaven: for in the like manner did their fathers unto the prophets" (Luke 6:22, 23).

Loving Enemies and Doing Good: "But love ye your enemies, and do good, and lend, hoping for nothing again; and your *reward* shall be great, and ye shall be the children of the Highest: for he is kind unto the unthankful and to the evil" (Luke 6:35).

Building Abiding Work: "If any man's work abide which he hath built thereupon, he shall receive a *reward*" (1 Cor. 3:14).

Preaching the Gospel Willingly: "For though I preach the gospel, I have nothing to glory of: for necessity is laid upon me; yea, woe is unto me, if I preach not the gospel! For if I do this thing willingly, I have a *reward:* but if against my will, a dispensation of the gospel is committed unto me" (1 Cor. 9:16, 17).

Doing Everything Heartily, as to the Lord: "And whatsoever ye do, do it heartily, as to the Lord, and not unto men; Knowing that of the Lord ye shall receive the *reward* of the inheritance: for ye serve the Lord Christ" (Col. 3:23, 24).

The rewards God will give to faithful Christians are called crowns. The New Testament mentions five of them. Those who receive them will cast them at the feet of the Lord (Rev. 4:10, 11). Jesus warned us, "Behold, I come quickly: hold that fast which thou hast, that no man take thy crown" (Rev. 3:11). The question is asked: Can another person steal our crowns, our rewards? No, the only way we can lose our reward is by default, not theft. That which we do for the Lord that meets the test of the Judgment Seat of Christ is ours and cannot be taken from us. However, we have many opportunities to serve the Lord, and if we do not use them, we lose them by default and consequently lose the rewards we could have had.

We can also lose rewards by living a careless and selfish life, and our works will be burned at the Judgment Seat of Christ.

John gave us two reasons for abiding in the Lord: "And now, little children, abide in him; that, when he shall appear, we may have confidence, and not be ashamed before him at his coming" (1 John 2:28).

John wanted us to have confidence when Christ comes; and, second, he did not want us to be ashamed at His coming. Then, in his second epistle, he expressed another concern: "Look to yourselves, that we lose not those things which we have wrought, but that we receive a full reward" (2 John 8).

"Look to yourselves" means "take heed" or "beware."

> It matters how we live, since what is done on earth will have its effect in eternity. Just as the servant who buried his one talent in the earth and the one who wrapped up his one talent in a napkin suffered permanent loss, so will the slothful and indolent Christian not only experience the loss of reward at the *bema*, but also be deprived for eternity of what he might have attained. . . . What we are now determines what we shall be for all eternity.[2]

May the LORD help us to listen to John's exhortation and receive a "full reward." "The Lord recompense thy work, and a full reward be given thee of the LORD God of Israel, under whose wings thou art come to trust" (Ruth 2:12).

HIS PLAN FOR ME

When I stand at the Judgment Seat of Christ,
And He shows me His plan for me,
The plan of my life as it might have been
Had He had His way, and I see

How I blocked Him here, and I checked Him there,
And I would not yield my will,
Will there be grief in my Saviour's eyes,
Grief, though He loves me still?

He would have me rich, and I stand there poor,
Stripped of all but His grace,

While memory runs like a hunted thing
Down the paths I cannot retrace.

Then my desolate heart will well-nigh break
With the tears I cannot shed;
I shall cover my face with my empty hands,
I shall bow my uncrowned head.

Lord, of the years that are left to me,
I give them to Thy hand;
Take me, break me, and mold me
To the pattern Thou hast planned.

—Martha Snell Nicholson

THE FIVE CROWNS

The clearest writing I have seen concerning the five crowns is a chapter in *The Judgment Seat of Christ* by Dr. L. Sale-Harrison. The following chapter is an adaptation of that discussion.[1]

We have clearly seen from the Word of God that the Judgment Seat of Christ is the place where rewards and losses are revealed. The losses have been explained, so we now come to the joyful and encouraging side of our subject—the rewards.

"*When the Lord comes* . . . He will expose the counsels of the heart and then shall every man have his own praise of God" (paraphrase of 1 Cor. 4:5). We connect this with 1 Corinthians 3:14: "If any man's work abide which he hath built thereupon, he shall receive a reward."

Even in the last message on rewards in the book of Revelation, we find that rewards are closely connected with the coming of the Lord. The same is true in 1 Corinthians 4:5. Only when the Lord comes will every Christian have his own praise of God. Therefore the Judgment Seat of Christ cannot take place now; it must be in the future.

I will enumerate the different rewards, and I hope that they will stimulate the fainting heart and discouraged soul.

The apostles mention in their epistles five crowns as rewards.

THE RUNNER'S CROWN

When Paul wrote to the Corinthians, he had in mind the old Isthmian games. He stated:

Know ye not that they which run in a race run all [all run], but one receiveth the prize? So run, that ye may obtain. And every man that striveth for the mastery is temperate [in self-control] in all things. Now they do it to obtain a *corruptible crown*; but we an *incorruptible*. I therefore so run, not as uncertainly; so fight I, not as one that beateth the air: But I keep under my body, and bring it into subjection: lest that by any means, when I have preached to others, I myself should be a castaway [not approved] (1 Cor. 9:24–27).

The apostle was speaking of the Christian race and the Christian warfare. "When I am running," he said, "I am keeping my eye on the goal; and in the fight I am not beating the air, I am fighting a real antagonist. I keep my own body under and beat it into subjection—making it my slave—lest that by any means when I have heralded the gospel to others, I myself should be a castaway (rejected in the race)." He does not mean castaway from his faith; this idea is not in the slightest way suggested.

His salvation is *not* brought into question at all. It is his race and warfare that he was explaining. The Greek word translated "castaway" is *adokimos,* meaning "not approved"—in the race. It is a word that was used in the Grecian games, and it really means "not worthy of the prize."

Verse 25 also states that the contestants in these Greek games brought themselves into complete control and abstained from anything that would check their activities.

In Sale-Harrison's young days in New Zealand many of the young folk trained for swimming, rowing and running. If there were a race on—especially a swimming race—for weeks beforehand they did not eat pastry sweets (candy, cakes, etc.). No matter how much the contestants enjoyed the sweets, they could not be persuaded to break their abstemious habits—though they usually made up for it later.

Paul then said: "They do it to obtain a corruptible crown, but we an incorruptible."

What was the big prize to the winner in Greece? Forty thousand dollars for a season? Many call that professionalism and not sport. Did those in Greece receive a heavy laden purse? No! That was beneath their dignity. They wanted to win the championship.

At the right time the champions came to the bema seat, where the umpire sat, and received from his hands a wreath of laurel leaves. To them the wreath was a sign of honor. What dignity was bestowed upon them in the parade! They were champions! The populace did not note the worth of the material composing the wreaths. They saw only the worth of the men who were worthy to wear those honors.

Paul said that men would go through a great deal to be crowned with this *perishable wreath;* but he also suggests the question, "What are we willing to suffer and bear for Christ to obtain an *incorruptible crown?*" Can we compare the value of this fleeting honor, given to the Grecian heroes, with the eternal worth of that which the faithful runner receives at the hands of his Lord?

Christ Himself stated to one who was prepared to follow Him later on: "No man, having put his hand to the plough, and looking back, is fit for the kingdom of God" (Luke 9:62).

How many times do we look back and allow things to come in that impede our progress? Not willing to deny self for Christ and the work's sake? Often more interested in how another is getting on and forgetting our own race?

In his younger days Dr. Sale-Harrison was in a swimming race representing a large number of swimmers. According to the speed of all the contestants, he should have won; but just as they neared the finishing mark, he heard the cheering and was anxious to see how the second-speed man behind him was getting on. The turn of his body stopped half a stroke. Almost immediately the two were at the finish. Their hands touched, but the other's was one-fifth of a second sooner. The race was lost because, in his eagerness, Sale-Harrison thought about the other man and not the goal. He took his mind off the task.

How many of us have done the same thing? Let us strain with earnestness every nerve, for we have not only a race to run but also a fight to wage. Paul spoke of this fight in Ephesians 6:12 and 13:

> For we wrestle not against flesh and blood, but against principalities, against powers, against the rulers of the darkness of this world [age],

against spiritual wickedness in high places. Wherefore take unto you the whole armour of God, that ye may be able to withstand in the evil day, and having done all, to stand.

Paul referred to a spiritual fight. We need to be equipped with the whole armor of God. How can we succeed unless we use spiritual weapons?

We must therefore note that this race, if well run, is one in which we put forth every effort and strain every nerve. Every fiber of one's spiritual being must be brought into play. There is no room for drones. Let us go to the ant, consider her ways and be wise (Prov. 6:6).

If Paul, in the height of spiritual manhood, said: "I keep under my body, and bring it into subjection" (1 Cor. 9:27), how can we win unless we do the same?

Peter said, "Gird up the loins of your mind" (1 Pet. 1:13).

The contestant in the race girded his garments around him. Nothing could impede his progress. He kept his eye on the goal. Let us then with enthusiasm run the race, keeping our eyes upon our Lord, so that we may receive at His hands the runner's crown.

THE SOUL-WINNER'S CROWN

The apostle Paul wrote to the Thessalonians: "For what is our hope, or joy, or *crown of rejoicing?* Are not even ye in the presence of our Lord Jesus Christ at His coming? For ye are our glory and joy" (1 Thess. 2:19, 20).

The writer was referring to those he had won for Christ. He stated that in the presence of our Lord Jesus Christ at His coming, those who were his children in Christ would be his crown of rejoicing, his hope, and his joy.

This is one of the Scriptures that I would use to convince others that we will know one another in glory. Paul says that it is when he sees his converts there that he will know them. They will be his crown of boasting. How could they be unless he was able to recognize them? We will certainly know one another in Heaven.

How many have you won for Christ? How many have you spoken to of the Lord? Your business and mine is to be soul-winners.

How appropriate are the wise man's words: "The fruit of the righteous is a tree of life; and he that winneth souls is wise" (Prov. 11:30).

Christ's words in Luke 15:10 reflect the value of a human soul in God's sight: "I say unto you there is joy in the presence of the angels of God over *one* sinner that repenteth."

When an unconverted person stands before us, do we realize that if this soul puts his or her trust in Christ, the bells of Heaven ring? The fact that our Lord came from Heaven to die an awful death upon the cross proves those choice words that He gave to Nicodemus: "For God so loved the world, that he gave his only begotten Son, that whosoever believeth in him should not perish, but have everlasting life" (John 3:16).

It is unsurprising, therefore, that Paul could look forward to the day of our Lord's appearing and see those who had trusted Christ through him, and with gladness say, "Ye are our crown of rejoicing!" What a joy this will be to Paul—and not only to him but to all who are earnest soul-seekers.

If the winning of a soul is exceedingly precious in God's sight, we need to live constantly near the Lord so that we may always be ready to deliver our message.

We must continually bear in mind that *unless* we love the Word of God and continually meditate upon it, we will not be great soul-winners. The Holy Spirit uses the Word to convict, although He can use His Word in spite of the instrument.

We have all seen that the worker who makes the Word of God his own usually wins souls. We see this fact especially in missionary activity. The societies that are being the most richly blessed—particularly in heathen lands—are those that demand of their missionaries a working knowledge of the Scriptures. The result is marvelous: Many rare trophies of the cross are won, and multitudes are added to the Church by these Bible-loving agents of the gospel.

What a reward will also be ours in that day if we, by loving God's Word, become earnest in our personal work for Christ.

THE LOVER'S CROWN

Is it not true that the times we live in make it extremely difficult for Christians to keep near the Lord? Trials, and often persecutions, continue to increase on every hand. Lawlessness is rapidly assuming alarming proportions, and the faith of the children of God is being tested severely.

Has not the Lord told us in His Word that these conditions would come in the latter days? If we have been studying the Scriptures, satanic advance has not caused us any surprise.

The Lord Jesus told His disciples (and, therefore, told us also) that "In the world ye shall have tribulation: but be of good cheer; I have overcome the world" (John 16:33) and that "I am with you alway, even unto the end of the [age]" (Matt. 28:20).

Is it not comforting to know that we are not left to assume our charges alone? God is always with us; therefore, we can take comfort as we realize by faith that He always manifests His presence.

One of the most encouraging Scriptures is found in James 1:12: "Blessed is the man that endureth temptation [trial]: for when he is tried [stood the test], he shall receive a *crown of life,* which the Lord hath promised to them that love him."

When one first reads this verse, he wonders what the apostle meant. James stated that the man who *"endures trial"* will receive a crown of life; then he immediately follows with the additional statement that the Lord has promised this crown to those who *"love"* Him.

What has "loving Him" to do with "enduring trial"? It is here that we see the beauty of the verse. Dr. Sale-Harrison answered this query by giving two illustrations.

While he was holding a Bible conference in a large church on the West Coast of the United States, the associate minister pointed out a man and a woman in the congregation. He asked, "What is your impression of those two from the look on their faces?" Sale-Harrison and his associates immediately answered, "They look exceedingly morose." He then related this story:

> Those two are members of this church. They are wealthy and have
> bestowed their love on their son—their only child. They have given

him a good education with the hope that he would take over his father's business and carry on the family's good name. Three months ago he became ill and died. They told the Lord that He should not have taken their son, because he was their only child. Rebellion has robbed them of their joy and peace. Though they are unaware of the gravity of their sin, really they have blamed the Lord for their son's death.

This example does not show "enduring trial." The parents needed to see that "all things work together for good to them that love God" and that even in that tragedy the Lord's wise hand was moving in their affairs, though they did not know it.

There can be no *crown of life* for such believers when the Lord comes.

The second illustration occurred during the First World War.

Every month in Australia the godly ministers and leading Christian workers of Dr. Sale-Harrison's district met for a time of fellowship. On one of these Monday mornings a dear friend of his—a brother minister—came in with an ashen face. He then told his story:

> I received a pink telegram this morning. [It is necessary to state that when a soldier or a nurse at the front was killed, wounded, sick, missing or had become a prisoner, an urgent telegram—pink in color—was sent by the government to the nearest minister. His duty was to break the news to the loved ones.] I walked across the carpet of my vestry [study] for an hour in agonizing prayer before I could be sure that I had courage to break the news to one of my loyal members who was a widow. At last I ventured out and went toward her house. While I was walking up the path, the door opened, and this bright little mother said cheerfully, "Come in, Pastor. I know you have some news for me. I felt it this morning when I was at prayer."

> I went into the drawing room and stood motionless, unable to speak. (This dear woman had several sons at the front. They were the only family she had.) She then turned to me and said, "Pastor, tell me, tell me." I still could not speak. Then seeing my face, in agony of soul she cried, "Pastor, which one, which one?"

I answered, "ALL." They had been in the same battalion. A barrage of German poison-gas shells came. Out of twelve hundred men, only twenty-seven were left alive.

This little mother looked stunned and then said, "Pastor, isn't it wonderful! The Lord gave me the joy of winning them all for Jesus, and I shall see them again when He comes."

Later she said to me, "Pastor, give me something to do to help others." I appointed her there and then as a visitor to those who had loved-ones at the front.

Dr. Sale-Harrison and the others met their ministerial friend several weeks later, and he told them this further story:

For three weeks I could not even mention the loss to this dear mother. When we met, I simply shook her hand. The tragedy was too sad and too deep to speak of it. After this period, I said to her, "Sister, I am so anxious to know how you are getting on."

She replied in these words, "Pastor, it was a terrible shock, and I wanted to be busy so that I would not have time to brood. I have visited the homes of mothers, wives, including the fiancées, and sisters who have lost their own loved ones. One dear mother whose only boy was killed said to me in anguish of soul, 'What do you know about losing a boy?' I made her sit down and quickly answered her: 'Dear mother, I know, for I lost all mine in one barrage of shells!' She could not cry before this; and as she looked at my face, she broke down in tears, and I was able to lead her to Jesus."

Then she said, "Pastor, this has been the greatest trial I have ever known; but the Lord has stood by me, and I love Him just the same."

Oh, yes! We can now see the beauty of our text and the connection between *"enduring temptation"* and *"love."* To make the explanation simple, Dr. Sale-Harrison paraphrased James 1:12 as follows: "Blessed is the man that endureth temptation: for when he is proved, he shall receive a crown of life, which the Lord hath promised to them *that love Him in spite of the trial."*

This dear mother in the second illustration above was the means of winning many souls for Christ. The crown of James 1:12 will one day be hers. You can certainly call this reward the "lover's crown," for only one who really loves Christ in spite of circumstances like these can be called a true lover of the Lord Jesus.

THE SHEPHERD'S, OR PASTOR'S, CROWN

If the faithful undershepherd, or pastor, is especially precious to the Lord, then we naturally expect that He will have a special reward for him. This is promised in 1 Peter 5:4: "When the chief Shepherd shall appear, ye shall receive a *crown of glory* that fadeth not away."

This unfading crown of glory is given only when the conditions outlined in the previous verses are fulfilled. What are these conditions?

The undershepherds were to shepherd the flock of God eagerly, not for base gain. Moreover, they were not to be autocratic dictators but models to the flock.

The danger exists that someone might accept the honorable position of spiritual leader as he would accept a business position— looking upon it as a mere profession and not as a call from God. One of the saddest things today is the commercializing of the ministry.

The Holy Spirit inspired Peter and Jude to write of Balaam, the false prophet, whose mind was clouded by the promised reward of the wicked king of Moab (see 2 Peter 2:15; Jude 11). May the Lord preserve us from even the suggestion of a commercial spirit in that which is designated spiritual service.

Should we deliberate upon an invitation because of the expected financial consideration or rather whether it is the leading of the Holy Spirit? Are we working for today or for tomorrow? Do we carry on our ministry in view of the Judgment Seat of Christ or in view of how much money we can lay aside for a rainy day?

We can understand why a person who has financial stress would be delighted when his faithful wife and children can live in comfort and receive things they really need because God's stewards are shouldering their responsibilities. Yet it is impossible for a Christian worker to call his life one of faith because he has no fixed salary while at the same time he shows an absence of daily trust in his Lord.

We are often put to shame by missionaries who go into the midst of heathenism, placing their absolute confidence in the Lord for their every need. No doubt the blackness of heathenism is the dark background that drives them to the mercy seat.

A young minister pleased Sale-Harrison one day with a simple recital of the leading of the Lord. He had been much blessed in a certain sphere, but he felt led to accept an invitation to minister in a more isolated community. His remuneration was smaller, but the opportunities in this new field were greater. The change meant a more careful husbanding of his family's resources; but his consecrated wife seconded his decision to say "yes." What was the result? The Lord began to use him as never before; many souls were saved and others were spiritually blessed. He said to us, "Does it not make one happy to know that he is in the will of the Lord?" This is the spirit of service that will find the reward in that day— *the unfading crown of glory.*

In meditating upon this phrase "fadeth not" (unfading), Dr. Sale-Harrison soon realized why such a word is used in the service of the undershepherd.

Is it not true that even a faithful man may be loved the first year and heralded as one of God's great servants in the second; while in the third year the church people become weary of him. Mass psychology is a poor foundation to rest upon. Even the love of Christians for their spiritual leaders can fade and change, but the crown of glory given to the worthy ones in that day *fadeth not.* What a contrast.

This encouraging word has helped many a dear pastor through discouragement and disappointment to continue quietly serving his Lord.

> It may not be on the mountain height,
> Or over the stormy sea;
> It may not be at the battle's front,

My Lord will have need of me;
But if by a still, small voice He calls
To paths that I do not know,
I'll answer, dear Lord, with my hand in Thine,
I'll go where you want me to go.

—*Mary Brown*

THE WATCHER'S CROWN

The second letter of Paul to Timothy was probably the last that he wrote before his death. Chapter 4 contains a tender message as Paul looked forward to martyrdom.

He told Timothy to preach the Word, for the time was coming when men would not tolerate wholesome instruction but would leave the truth and accept fables. This warning suggests that men would accept the modernists' version of the Scriptures, charging that the truth of God was only folklore (fables).

After these prophetic utterances, Paul gave a striking and touching appeal in the following words:

> But watch thou in all things, endure afflictions, do the work of an evangelist, make full proof of thy ministry. For I am now ready to be offered, and the time of my departure is at hand. I have fought a good fight, I have finished my course, I have kept the faith. Henceforth there is laid up for me a *crown of righteousness,* which the Lord, the righteous judge, shall give me at that day: and not to me only, but unto all them also that love his appearing (2 Tim. 4:5–8).

He said that because of his life and service, so gloriously lived for the Lord, a "crown of righteousness" was laid up for him in "that day." He had lived his life well; he had faithfully rendered his service; he had endured terrible persecutions. And through it all he had kept the faith. What a record! Few of us dare say what he could state.

Note how the Lord's appearing is again linked with the reward: "Which the Lord, the righteous judge, shall give me at that day: and not to me only, but unto all them also that *love his appearing.*"

It is wonderful to note that the one who loves the thought of Christ's appearing is to receive the same reward as Paul, who had lived such a marvelous life for the Lord, giving up everything for Him. How important then is our trust in the truth of the appearing of Christ.

God never commences anything that He does not intend to finish. His plans are never left half-baked. He is a God of order and a God of purpose. He is completing the Church—He must complete it—and one day the last member will be ushered in, closing this dispensation of grace. It is then that the shout of the Lord and the trump of God will call us to meet Him in the air (see 1 Thess. 4:16, 17).

Seeing that we have the Lord's return given so often in the Scriptures, nearly four hundred times in the New Testament alone, how can we ignore its appeal? And if we love the Lord Jesus, we surely are eager to see Him.

Would it not be strange to have so many Biblical passages appealing to us to "watch lest we be found sleeping," if there were no blessings to be given as a reward? It is certain that the watcher—the one who does all his work in light of that return—pleases the Lord much more than the sleeper.

We believe that the whole Church will be caught up to be with the Lord in the air. But this Scripture also proves that a special *victor's crown of righteousness* will be given to all those who love His appearing.

William R. Featherstone probably had this crown in mind when he composed these beautiful lines:

> In mansions of glory and endless delight,
> I'll ever adore Thee in heaven so bright;
> I'll sing with the glittering crown on my brow,
> If ever I loved Thee, my Jesus, 'tis now.

LOSS AT THE JUDGMENT SEAT OF CHRIST

Some people do not seem to realize there will be loss at the Judgment Seat of Christ. Or they think that if there is loss, it will not be serious. One well-known pastor said:

> The first thing Jesus will do when He comes for His church is to reward His people for their service. We will be able to go before the judgment seat of Christ with absolute confidence. How can we have that confidence? Because we are saved. . . .
>
> Verse 10 [2 Cor. 5:10] adds that everyone will receive a reward— no one will be ashamed. . . .
>
> Every individual at the judgment seat of Christ will have praise from God. There is no shame for anyone.
>
> The bema . . . serves only for giving out rewards.[1]

In an article in *Good News Broadcaster* the same pastor wrote: "Because Romans 6:8 [*sic*, 6:14] says that we are not under law, what are we under? We are under grace. There is no way that any sin in the life of a Christian is unforgiven."[2]

Wayne Sutton commented on this statement: "Such travesties of logic need to be carefully avoided, and point out the possibility that one's deeply held presuppositions may disguise the inadequacy of his arguments."[3]

In this chapter I include the writings of a number of prophetic scholars concerning the negative aspects of the Judgment Seat of Christ.

Samuel L. Hoyt wrote in *Bibliotheca Sacra*: "To overdo the sorrow aspect of the judgment seat of Christ is to make heaven hell. To underdo the sorrow aspect is to make faithfulness inconsequential."[4]

I desire to make Heaven Heaven and faithfulness consequential.

The next section, Tears in Heaven—which includes The Testimony of Scripture, The Testimony of Bible Expositors and The Testimony of Human Experience—has been adapted from a sermon by John Linton.[5]

TEARS IN HEAVEN

In July 1940 a group of about forty Bible teachers met at the Moody Bible Institute for a private conference on prophecy. On the second day a well-known minister arrived late and took his place in the group. He said he had come many miles to find the answer to one question. He quoted Matthew 25:30, which tells about the unprofitable servant who was cast into outer darkness. The verse goes on to say, "There shall be weeping and gnashing of teeth." He said in effect, "I have members in my church who are unprofitable servants. They live on the low levels of the Christian life. They are prayerless, indifferent and worldly but are resting on the fact that salvation is by grace and once saved they can never be lost. I know I need a message from God to arouse my unfaithful members. To tell them of a limited reward in Heaven means nothing to them. To get into Heaven is all they desire. I need a message, brethren, with teeth in it. If you men will tell me this unfaithful servant who weeps and gnashes his teeth is a Christian in Heaven, I believe I have the message that some of my people need."

That question was never answered for lack of time, but some weeks later Linton wrote that pastor and said, "I may not know the meaning of the verse you quote, but if you will invite me to preach to your people, I will give them from other Scriptures the message you want and they need."

In 2 Corinthians 5:10 we read, "For we [Christians] must all appear before the judgment seat of Christ; that every one may receive the things done in his body, according to that he hath done, whether it be good or bad." What a startling, stupendous, soul-gripping statement. Christians will receive in Heaven not only a reward for obedience but a recompense for disobedience. We are familiar with the reward for faithfulness, but whoever thinks of a recompense for unfaithfulness? But there it is in God's Word. I dare you to explain it away, "That every one may receive the things done in his body—whether it be good or bad."

Have you noticed that while there is only one door to Heaven, there are two different ways by which we can enter that door. Here is one way, "Well done good and faithful servant: enter thou into the joy of thy Lord." Here is the same way in other words, "For if ye do these things . . . an entrance shall be ministered unto you abundantly into the everlasting kingdom." Note the phrases "well done" and "abundant entrance." They describe one way of entering.

Now here is another way of entering Heaven. *"Ashamed before him at his coming"* (1 John 2:28). And again, *"saved yet so as by fire"* (1 Cor. 3:15). Question: If a Christian stands ashamed in the presence of Christ, will he be happy or sad? Will he be laughing or weeping?

And not only is our manner of entrance into Heaven decided, but our position and privileges there are also determined by our faithfulness. The servant who faithfully used his five talents was made ruler over five cities. The servant faithful with two talents was made ruler over two cities. Their heavenly position and privileges were determined by their earthly faithfulness.

The story is told of a contractor who built a house for a rich friend. He skimped on the work wherever it would pass unnoticed. He put cheap material into the foundation where it would not for some years be revealed. It looked imposing, but it was unsubstantial and unsafe. When he had finished the house, his rich friend handed it over to him as a personal gift so that, to his utter discomfiture, he inherited the fruit of his own unfaithfulness. In robbing his friend he had robbed himself. So also is the resurrection of the dead. The money that we kept back from God, and that could have added to our eternal joy, will be one cause of our shame and loss and tears in Heaven.

Yes, there is to be a judgment for Christians in Heaven, both for reward and for recompense. The Bible does not picture Christians without any responsibility for their stewardship "sweeping through the gates of the New Jerusalem" and tripping gaily into a Heaven of equal bliss. Our capacity for enjoying Heaven we take to Heaven with us. Although we shall not meet in Heaven our sin that is repented of and forgiven, yet we shall meet its consequences. Our unfaithfulness to Christ here will limit our capacity for enjoying Christ yonder. Thus the sins of the saints, though confessed and forgiven, will have unending consequences in an everlasting limitation of joy.

After the Judgment Seat is over and each Christian's place is allotted him, he shall be perfected; and God, I believe, will blot out the remembrance of past failure and wipe away all tears from our eyes. Then we shall all be fully happy—but not equally happy. This fountain pen is full and an ocean is full, but what a vast difference between the respective capacities of this tiny pen and the mighty deep. So also is the resurrection of the dead.

Then Linton presented three lines of proof to corroborate what he had just said.

THE TESTIMONY OF SCRIPTURE

The judgment of Christians for reward and recompense is consistently taught in many passages.

Take 1 Corinthians 4:5: "Judge nothing before the time, until the Lord come, who both will bring to light the hidden things of darkness, and will make manifest the counsels of the hearts: and then shall every man have praise of God." This passage teaches that God keeps a record of the hidden things among Christians and will bring them to light when the record is read. What we cover up, God will uncover. What we hide, God will reveal in that day.

Look at Colossians 3:23–25: "And whatsoever ye do, do it heartily, as to the Lord . . . knowing that of the Lord ye shall receive the reward of the inheritance: for ye serve the Lord Christ. But he that doeth wrong shall receive for the wrong which he hath done: and there is no respect of persons." Here Paul plainly declared that Christians will be recompensed for wrongdoing. What that recompense is Paul did not say, and I do not know.

Consider also 1 Corinthians 3:14 and 15: "If any man's work abide which he hath built thereupon, he shall receive a reward. If any man's work shall be burned, he shall suffer loss: but he himself shall be saved; yet so as by fire." Here we are told the unfaithful Christian will suffer loss. Is it nothing to suffer loss? Linton said, "I am not making a play on words when I ask, Does not 'suffer loss' mean to suffer? Is it nothing for a Christian to be 'saved yet so as through a fire'?"

In Romans 14:10–12 we read, "Why dost thou judge thy brother? or why dost thou set at nought thy brother? for we shall all stand before the judgment seat of Christ. For it is written, As I live, saith the Lord, every knee shall bow to me, and every tongue shall confess to God. So then every one of us shall give account of himself to God." This is one of the misapplied passages of the Bible. Christians apply it only to the unsaved who will have to acknowledge Christ as God in eternity. But that is only one application of this Old Testament promise. The primary application is to Christians at the Judgment Seat of Christ. There God has a confessional—not a private box but a public confessional—and every sin among Christians not dealt with down here will be dealt with up yonder. "Every tongue shall confess" means every tongue, including the tongues of stubborn and unrepentant Christians.

The apostle John told us plainly there will be shame in Heaven for Christians. He said in 1 John 2:28, "And now, little children, abide in him; that, when he shall appear, we may have confidence, and not be ashamed before him at his coming." As plain as language can put it, John stated that Christians who do not abide will stand covered with shame. Question: When the Christian stands ashamed, will he have a smile on his face or tears in his eyes?

THE TESTIMONY OF BIBLE EXPOSITORS

That leads to a second line of proof—the testimony of Bible expositors.

The teaching of rewards and recompense for Christians is not new. It has been taught for centuries. It is a truth that has sometimes been obscured and neglected because of our emphasis on the glorious grace of God that gives eternal life to every sinner who believes. But the two do not contradict each other. Grace brings us into God's family; how we behave there is what the Judgment Seat of Christ will deal with.

Donald Grey Barnhouse, in a masterly and comprehensive sermon on this subject, pointed out how believers are justified by grace, given the prerogative of sonship purely by grace, granted the gift of eternal life by grace so that our position in God's family is secure and apart from human merit. Then he added:

> Nevertheless, in spite of all this, there is a sense in which our deeds have an effect that is an eternal effect. The thief on the cross had a life that was wasted, and coming to Christ in the moment of his death he was saved and is in Heaven, but it is impossible to conceive that he shall ever hear the voice of the Lord saying, "Well done, thou good and faithful servant." Most certainly he was saved, "yet so as by fire" (1 Cor. 3:15). "We must all appear before the judgment seat of Christ" (2 Cor. 5:10). Let us not forget that fact.

B. H. Carroll, the great preacher of the South, speaking on the subject, "Inequality in Heaven," said,

> Compare the fidelity of two women in the same church. One with sweetest meekness and self-denial honors her Lord in all things. When the world and society offer her their carnal pleasures her questions are, What would my Lord have me to do? Will these develop my spiritual nature? Will they increase my Christian influence? She does not ask what harm is in them but what good? And so living in all things unto the Lord, ornamenting her life with good works, she finishes her course with joy, and her children rise up and call her blessed.

> Another indeed accepts the Lord as her Savior but ever lives with divided heart and service. The claims of the world, of society, are acknowledged more than the claims of Christ's cause. She follows Jesus afar off. Her heart is cold. She cannot be counted on for regular Christian work. Sinners through her are not convicted of sin and led

to repentance. She worships much at the shrines of pleasure and but seldom at the altars of God. In times of death and other great bereavement she remembers God, but her life on the whole has been, after all, but a shabby, ragged and miserable service. And so she passes away to the great judgment throne. The question recurs with emphasis: "Shall these two women find Heaven equal?"

And the answer to Dr. Carroll's question is plain: Rewards will be proportionate to fidelity, and rebuke will be forthcoming for unfaithfulness. Dr. Carroll's answer to his own question is, "Of course these two women will not find Heaven equal."

And yet another Bible commentator well stated:

> The world has a foolish idea of "Going to Heaven when we die": that is, to an indiscriminate Heaven of unvaried bliss, into which all Christians are swept irrespective of all else. Grace to such is merely another word for *irresponsibility.* Forgiveness wipes out everything—character, injustice, cruel and continuing wrongs, and leaves all on the dead level of no responsibility and no accountability. It's all right, for we go to Heaven; nothing else really matters. Let us fear lest we conceive the same folly in our hearts—man is never irresponsible. Grace does not relieve him of accountability. We must all appear before the judgment seat of Christ.

It was because he saw the everlasting consequence to the believer of obedience and disobedience that the great Bible expositor Dr. Alexander Maclaren said,

> I believe for my part that we suffer terribly by the comparative neglect into which this side of Christian truth has fallen. Do you not think that it would make a difference to you if you really believed, and carried away with you in your thoughts the thrilling consciousness that every act of the present was registered, and would tell on the far side beyond?

THE TESTIMONY OF HUMAN EXPERIENCE

Finally, this truth of reward and recompense for believers in Heaven is consistent with the testimony of human experience.

For one thing, *all Christians are not equally happy on earth.* Why should it be thought a thing incredible that the joy of Christians in Heaven is unequal, when joy among believers on earth is unequal? Do all Christians on earth find equal joy in contemplation of Christ? Of course not. Jesus Christ is present at the prayer meeting in every church week by week, but many of the members do not enjoy Him enough to attend.

Other Christians, because of lack of passion for the lost, because of prejudice against evangelists and evangelistic services, do not enter heartily into soul-winning effort. They have been known to oppose evangelistic meetings in their churches. Such a Christian dies. He goes to Heaven. He is not there five minutes before all Heaven bursts into praise. He asks one of the angels why they are rejoicing, and the angel answers, "There is joy in Heaven over one sinner that repents. A man has been saved on earth in an evangelistic meeting; a prodigal son has been saved in answer to a mother's prayers. That is why everybody up here is happy." How will that man feel?

Some Christians turn up on Sunday morning at the end of a week of soul-winning services in their church. They have been absent all week. Other Christians are walking on air with joy over sinners saved. The angels are rejoicing. The Father in Heaven rejoiced to see the prodigal coming home. The Good Shepherd, as He brought home the lost sheep on His shoulders, rejoiced. But these indifferent church members were not there. Like the elder brother they were absent when the prodigal returned. They are out of sympathy with the happy servants and the rejoicing father. Well, will they suddenly go into ecstasies over saved sinners when they get to Heaven? Who will give them this sudden interest? Will the undertaker change them? Will the funeral sermon make them different? Nothing is more reasonable and consistent with human experience than the truth that every day is a judgment day, and we are deciding today the kind of Heaven we shall enter tomorrow.

Moreover, *all matters are not being righteously judged.* It will be necessary for matters among Christians to be judged in Heaven, for they are not judged equitably here. Many questions have to be answered and wrongs righted.

Charles Spurgeon was censured by a vote of the Baptist Union of Great Britain for opposing the inroads of modernism. Who was right in that act? Was it Mr. Spurgeon or the ministers who censured him? God will make that known at the Judgment Seat of Christ. That dispute, and many others, will be dealt with. God's holiness demands the righteous judgment of all unjudged or misjudged matters between the Christian and his Lord and the Christian and his fellow Christian.

And again, *all Christians are not equally faithful.* Although the most faithful Christian is still an unprofitable servant, nevertheless the difference among Christians in faithfulness is such that a righteous God will inevitably take note of this difference.

Think of the difference in separation. Some young people keep their garments unspotted from the world. They shun the very appearance of evil. If a thing is even questionable, they give it up for Christ's sake and for the sake of weaker Christians. Others, alas, do not think of the Lord or of others in such things. They try to hold on to the world's amusements with one hand and to Christ with the other. When it is a choice between the house of prayer and the house of pleasure, the Lord has to take second place. It is reasonable and inevitable as well as Scriptural that God observes this difference. A spiritual joy is reserved for the separated Christian but denied to those whose garments have been spotted by the pleasures of the world.

There is a difference also in soul winning. What zeal, what passion, what earnestness marks the efforts of some to lead souls to Christ in contrast with the indifference and selfishness of others.

In a certain church Linton had urged Christians to win souls. A young woman responded by earnestly asking God to give her power to win someone to Christ during the meetings. By the end of two weeks she had led six young women to Christ. But several hundred other Christians heard the same sermon; and not only did they not win one soul, they did not even try. This difference in soul-winning zeal will add to the joy of the earnest Christian and bring regret to the lazy, selfish believer in that day.

Then, too, there is a manifest difference in sacrificial giving. Here are two happenings that occurred in the same church illustrating the difference among Christians in giving. A railway fireman was a member of a church in Montreal where Linton later became pastor. One day while eating lunch at a railway siding he asked the engineer on his train this question, "What do you think of Jesus Christ?"

The engineer bluntly replied, "I don't think very much of Jesus Christ. You see, my wife is a member of your church. I give her my paycheck every half month. I make good money, and we are comfortably well off. My wife can do what she likes with that money, for I never ask her to tell me how she spends it. I happen to know that she puts in her church collection ten cents each Sunday." Pointing to a small bag of biscuits in his hand the engineer continued, "This bag of biscuits cost me ten cents. You ask me what I think of Jesus Christ. I figure it this way. If Jesus Christ is worth no more than the price of a ten-cent bag of biscuits, I reckon I can afford to live without Him."

Here was an unsaved man who was taking what his wife put in the offering plate as her estimate of the value of Christ, and her lack of sacrificial giving was keeping her husband from God.

How vastly different from another family in that same church during Linton's pastorate there. They were the poorest of the poor, yet they gave to the Lord. One day, as Linton visited their humble home, the woman said, "Pastor, you are just in time to pray with us. We are going out this week to look for a smaller house. We do not need these five rooms, which cost us eighteen dollars monthly. We can live nicely in three rooms. There are just three of us: my husband, my boy and myself. If God will help us get a smaller house at a lower rent, we will give the difference to His work." Linton tried to pray that God would guide them in search of a cheaper house.

The next Sunday the woman was radiant. They had found a house at twelve dollars per month. They would have six dollars more a month to give to Jesus Christ!

Linton described that house: It was on the poorest street in the district. It had three small rooms. There wasn't a carpet on the floor. When he would visit them and, on leaving, kneel to pray, the husband would say, "Wait a minute, Pastor." Then he would slip a newspaper under Linton's knees so that he would not be kneeling on a bare floor. It was spotlessly white, but quite bare.

There wasn't a chair in the house. There were things that looked like chairs, but if you had turned them upside down, you would have seen they were only old boxes with boards nailed up the back and covered over with old tapestry to look like chairs and thus deceive the very elect. One cold Canadian winter day when Linton took a returned missionary from India to their home because he wanted to thank them personally for their gifts to him, the poor missionary nearly froze, for there wasn't a bit of fire in the grate. They were saving money for their beloved Lord and His missionaries.

Living in this three-room house, earning together (for both husband and wife worked) the sum of twenty-seven dollars weekly, they went to a missionary conference and pledged a certain amount to missions. They were given all the time they wanted to redeem their pledge. They cheerfully made it. How much did they give from the deepest poverty to that one particular offering? The sum of seven hundred dollars! Linton reported, "I know that is true, because I was there when the pledge was paid."

Now will you tell me God will not make a difference between these two women in Heaven? One gave of her plenty—ten cents per week. The other gave of her poverty—seven hundred dollars to missions. If the generosity of one Christian will bring joy, the meanness of another will bring regret. Experience says it must be, and God's Word says it will be.

Linton concluded by urging every saved man and woman reading his message to get right with God and get right with man: If you know of a wrong to be righted, do it dear friend, while yet there is time. If you have an unconfessed sin, confess it this side of the Judgment Seat. Don't spoil that first interview with Christ by having to be rebuked for unfaithfulness.

GETTING READY TO MEET THE JUDGE

The following discussion is an adaptation from *Grace in Eclipse* by Zane C. Hodges.[6]

There is no more lovely doctrine in Scripture than the doctrine of God's matchless grace. But in some quarters of Christendom that superlative theme has been stretched almost beyond recognition. Grace will indeed play a significant role at the judgment of believers. Who has ever accomplished anything apart from its enabling? But the Judgment Seat of Christ is a place where the Christian's *performance* comes into view. And therefore the question of merit comes into view as well.

Not to maintain this balance with regard to the Biblical doctrine of judgment is to invite—yes, to *assure*—the distortion of much Scripture.

ACCOUNTABILITY

We Christians have an urgent need, therefore, for a renewed recognition of our accountability—not the kind of pseudo-accountability, however, that is so frequently hawked in the religious marketplace today.

The Christian is *not* in danger of losing his eternal salvation. Every believer in Christ not only has eternal life but will still belong to Christ when he is raised up at the last day (John 6:37–40). No one who has ever drunk of the water of life will ever be thirsty for that water again (John 4:13, 14).

Neither is the Christian's accountability to be held hostage to a distorted presentation of the gospel or to some subtle reshaping of the concept of saving faith.

A Christian's accountability is just that. He is saved freely and forever by the grace of God. But once he has been saved, he is profoundly responsible for what he does with the rest of his life.

He can build his "house" on sand if he so chooses. But the "house" will collapse in ruins around him, and he will have to give an account of his folly before God. He can "save" his life if he chooses by self-interested living, but his life will actually be lost if he does. And he will have to give an account of this before God. He can hoard his material assets if he so decides, but to the degree that he does, he will impoverish himself in the world to come. And he will have to acknowledge his greed before God.

Scripture is plain: "As I live, says the Lord, every knee shall bow to me, and every tongue shall confess to God" (Rom. 14:11). That is accountability!

Some argue that the believer's sins cannot come under consideration at Christ's Judgment Seat since they are all forgiven. But this confuses the two kinds of judgment. The Christian's eternal destiny is not at issue in the judgment of believers; hence "sin" as a barrier to his entrance into eternal fellowship with God is not at issue either.

But it must be kept in mind that to review and assess a life, the Judge must consider the life in its entirety. And that obviously includes the bad with the good. Indeed, Paul told us this quite plainly when he wrote: "For we must all appear before the judgment seat of Christ; that every one may receive the things done in his body, according to that he hath done, *whether it be good or bad*" (2 Cor. 5:10; emphasis added).

That this thought was as solemn to Paul as it is to us is clear from his next words: "Knowing therefore the terror of the Lord, we persuade men" (2 Cor. 5:11).

GETTING READY TO MEET THE JUDGE

It behooves the Christian, therefore, to give the day of accounting some serious thought. Many cherish the illusion that unsavory secrets will always be just that—secrets between themselves and God. The Scriptures do not support this view of things.

Eternity has no secrets. Jesus Himself said so. In fact, while warning His disciples against the pretense so common among the religious leaders of His day, He said this:

> Beware ye of the leaven of the Pharisees, which is hypocrisy. For there is nothing covered, that shall not be revealed; neither hid, that shall not be known. Therefore whatsoever ye have spoken in darkness shall be heard in the light; and that which ye have spoken in the ear in closets shall be proclaimed upon the housetops (Luke 12:1–3).

The apostle Paul carried this a step further: "Therefore judge nothing before the time, until the Lord come, who will both bring to light the hidden things of darkness, and will *make manifest the counsels of the hearts:* and then shall every man have praise of God" (1 Cor. 4:5; emphasis added).

It is too early, said Paul, to judge anything properly. To do that, one would need to know not only the dark secrets of men but their *motives* as well. So wait until the Lord comes. Everything will be clear then! And when that happens, men will get whatever praise they truly deserve.

Therefore, since no human secret can remain a secret permanently, the Christian might well desire that the Day of Judgment should reveal more than "the hidden things of darkness." Why should it not also disclose secrets that are worthy of praise?

It will! And Jesus told us so in His Sermon on the Mount. In fact, one of His most motivating suggestions was this: "But when thou doest alms, let not thy left hand know what thy right hand doeth, That your alms may be in secret: and thy Father which seeth in secret himself shall *reward thee openly*" (Matt. 6:3, 4).

Shortly after, He also said this: "But thou, when thou prayest, enter into thy closet, and when thou hast shut thy door, pray to thy Father which is in secret; and thy Father which seeth in secret shall *reward thee openly*" (v. 6).

And a little later He added: "But thou, when thou fastest, anoint thine head, and wash thy face; That thou appear not unto men to fast, but unto thy Father which is in secret: and thy Father which seeth in secret, shall *reward thee openly*" (Matt. 6:17, 18; emphasis added).

What delightful secrets for a man to have—secret charities, secret prayers, secret fastings! Here surely are activities to be stored up in great quantity for that "day when God shall judge the secrets of men by Jesus Christ" (Rom. 2:16). And the reward for them—the "pay"—will be a recompense made in public!

That is one way for a Christian to get ready to meet his Judge. But there are other ways. In particular, as the thought of charitable deeds already suggests, one needs especially to be merciful. This was what James had in mind when he wrote that the one who has shown no mercy will be judged without mercy (James 2:13).

In saying this James was, of course, speaking to Christians who will be judged by Christian standards, all suitably summed up as "the law of liberty" (James 2:12). He had been addressing his readers as people who held "the faith of our Lord Jesus Christ, the Lord of glory," but who tended to mix this with an inappropriate partiality toward the rich (2:1). This attitude led to harsh, thought-less, unmerciful behavior toward the poor (2:2, 3), and it was a serious infraction of the royal law of Scriptures, "Thou shalt love thy neighbour as thyself" (2:8, 9).

"All right then," James said, "Just remember this. If you are an unmerciful person in your dealings with others, you must face a judgment untempered by mercy!"

This is an arresting thought! For what Christian can survey his earthly experience without sensing that when called to account, he wants to be treated with mercy? It is not a question of fearing the loss of salvation. That subject does not even enter the picture. But it is rather a question of being held strictly to the standards of God's Word and of having our recompense measured out in those demanding terms alone. No honest believer wants a judgment exactly like that!

But many Christians are rigid and uncompromising in their demands on others. In addition, they can be thoughtless, unfor-giving, unkind and even cruel. And if this has been their manner on earth—if mercy has not marked their dealings with others—mercy will not mark their own judgment either!

So to get ready to meet his Judge, the Christian should specialize in mercy. After all, said James, "Mercy [triumphs over] judgment" (2:13).

But—and it is close to being the same thing—the Christian should also specialize in love. Mercy was James's word. Love is John's.

We should expect that love would be John's word. He was "the disciple whom Jesus loved." He had leaned on Jesus' bosom and felt there the heartbeat of God. He was preeminently the apostle of love.

John believed firmly, of course, in the unconditional love of God, lavishly expressed in the giving of His Son that men might have eternal life. Naturally, no judgment lies ahead to test whether that love is still the believer's possession or not. A judgment like that is unthinkable!

But a judgment lies ahead to test the believer's works. "Behold I come quickly; and my reward is with me, to give every man according [to] his work," are words recorded by the apostle of love himself. John believed deeply in that sort of judgment.

And he also believed that such judgment could be fearful. Like Paul he knew "the terror of the Lord" (2 Cor. 5:11). Although this judgment *can* be fearful, it *need not* be. And the way to avoid the fear that that day could bring is *to love!*

No wonder then that the Scriptures lay such stress on how Christ will find us when He returns. We have already listened to John's words: "And now, little children, abide in him; that, when he shall appear, we may have confidence, and not be ashamed before him at his coming" (1 John 2:28).

And Peter also admonished us: "Wherefore, beloved, [looking forward to these] things, be diligent *[to] be found [by] him* in peace, without spot, and blameless" (2 Pet. 3:14; emphasis added).

But the most solemn warning of all was issued by the King Himself. On one occasion the Lord Jesus had spoken at length concerning the events surrounding His second advent. In the midst of the great exposition of future things—we call it the Olivet Discourse—the Son of God inserted a parable designed to warn and challenge His servants. He began the parable this way: "Who then is a faithful and wise servant, whom his lord hath made ruler over his household, to give them [food] in due season? Blessed is that servant whom his lord *when he cometh* shall find so doing. Verily I say unto you, That he shall make him ruler over all his goods" (Matt. 24:45–47; emphasis added).

Here again is co-heirship with the coming King. The servant who is faithfully performing his duties *when his Master arrives* is elevated to a position with sweeping authority: "He will make him ruler over all his goods."

But another outcome for this servant's career looms as a somber possibility:

> But and if that evil servant shall say in his heart, My lord delayeth his coming; And shall begin to [beat] his fellowservants, and to eat and drink with the drunken; the lord of that servant *shall come [on] a day when he looketh not* for him, and in an hour that he is not aware of, and shall cut him [in two], and *appoint him his portion with the hypocrites:* there shall be weeping and gnashing of teeth (Matt. 24:48–51; emphasis added).

Naturally, we must not suppose, as many have done, that our Lord spoke here of an unsaved man. He was still talking about the same individual whom he had just described as a potential ruler over His goods. The words, "But if *that* evil servant," make it plain.

Moreover, this wicked slave was *not* an unbeliever at all. He actually believed in the coming of his Lord but persuaded himself that this coming would be postponed: "My master is delaying his coming!" But this was his fatal error. No longer moved by a sense of watchfulness, his lifestyle degenerated rapidly. He began to mistreat his Christian brethren (his "fellowservants") and then to indulge himself with intemperate and base behavior. He ate and drank with the drunkards.

In this lamentable state of soul, the servant was utterly unprepared for his master's arrival and for the day of accounting that followed. Indeed, his judge cut him to pieces!

Of course, Jesus was dealing here in metaphor. The English rendering ("cut him in two") is too precise. The underlying Greek verb can signify "to cut something up," and it should be evident that this expression is a figure of speech. Not even unsaved people will ever be *literally* cut to pieces—how much less Jesus' own servants!

But the day of accounting is nonetheless dreadful for the unfaithful servant of Christ. The "terror of the Lord" will be, for such a man, only too real. And the instrument by which his failed life will be judged is sharp indeed:

> For the word of God is [living], and powerful, and sharper than any twoedged sword, piercing even to the [division] of soul and spirit, and of the joints and marrow, and is a discerner of the thoughts and intents of the heart. [And there is no creature hidden from] his sight: but all things are naked and opened unto the eyes of him *[to whom we must give an account]* (Heb. 4:12, 13; emphasis added).

No doubt, for the kind of man whom our Lord's parable describes, the Judgment Seat of Christ will seem like exquisitely painful surgery on his soul. The sharp, two-edged sword of the divine Word will "bring to light the hidden things of darkness, and will [reveal] the counsels of the hearts" (1 Cor. 4:5). Surely the agony of exposure will be indescribably acute.)

In addition to that is the loss of co-heirship with Christ. Instead—and the irony is powerful—there is co-heirship with hypocrites! For He will "appoint him his *portion* with the hypocrites. There shall be weeping and gnashing of teeth."

This servant had become a hypocrite—*not* a hypocrite in the sense that he only pretended to be a Christian. Such a thought is totally extraneous to this text. Instead, he had occupied the position and role of a servant of Christ and had ended by serving only himself. His role was ostensibly to feed his Lord's household, but instead he beat his fellow servants and indulgently fed himself. And that was hypocrisy! Profound regret was its rightful legacy.

Tragically, we have no reason to think that there will not be many such hypocrites standing at the Judgment Seat of Christ. Like the fearful servant in the parable of the minas (mites; one mina equaled 1/60 talent), they will hear their Lord's stinging rebuke, and it will be as though a two-edged sword pierced their innermost being. They will experience deep shame. They will weep and gnash their teeth.

This will not go on forever, of course. Indeed, perhaps it will be only for a short time, for ultimately God will wipe away all tears from their eyes (Rev. 21:4). But those who cannot conceive of a Christian grieving deeply over an unfaithful life and sorrowing profoundly over a lost heirship are not being realistic. In fact, it is precisely the glorified saint, free at last from the deluding influences of sin, who will likely be most moved with unutterable sadness over a life that has been poorly invested for God.)

THE MOST NEGLECTED ASPECT OF THE JUDGMENT SEAT OF CHRIST

This section is an adaptation of an article, "The Judgment Seat of Christ," by Thomas M. Meachum.[7]

The Scriptures state that it is appointed for men to die once, and afterward comes judgment (Heb. 9:27). This statement applies to *all* men—unbelievers and believers. A survey of the New Testament reveals that the judgment of men after death actually consists of two distinct judgments separated by at least a thousand years and differing from each other in many of their aspects. Either because of an overemphasis upon the judgment of the unsaved or the acceptance of the amillennial doctrine of a general resurrection and judgment, the Biblical teaching of a believer's judgment has been neglected or totally set aside to the point that many members of fundamental churches are ignorant of this most practical truth, an ignorance that they evidence by their lack of personal separation from the world.

The New Testament places just as much emphasis upon the judgment of believers as it does upon the judgment of unbelievers.

The New Testament reveals the purpose of the Judgment Seat of Christ. A judgment to determine one's final destiny is out of the question here; that issue was settled at the moment of salvation (Rom. 8:1). The mere fact that one stands before the Judgment Seat of Christ testifies to the fact of his salvation. First Corinthians 3:13 describes how each man's *work* will become evident when the fire of divine judgment will test the quality of each *work*. Second Corinthians 5:10 states the purpose of the Judgment Seat of Christ: that each one may be recompensed for his *deeds* "in his body, according to that he hath done, whether it be good or bad." The word here translated "bad" is *phaulos* and is more correctly translated "worthless." Trench stated that *phaulos* is a word that views ". . . evil under another aspect, not so much that either of active or passive malignity, but that rather of its good-for-nothingness, the impossibility of any gain ever coming forth from it." The evil "deeds" of the believer are sinful; they cannot be classified otherwise. Yet, while not denying their sinfulness, *phaulos* brings out the fact that they are viewed in regard to their lack of value in promoting the cause of Christ and the believer's standing in Heaven. Because such "deeds" are sinful (either because of their nature or the motive with which they were done), they are worthless to the believer when he stands before the Judgment Seat of Christ. The sin aspect of the "deeds" done by the believer since his salvation has already been taken care of, either by confession in this life resulting from varying degrees of chastisement or by the transformation that takes place at death.

The question of unconfessed sins, that is, those sins that the believer fails or refuses to confess even in the face of divine chastisement (Heb. 12:5–11), has been raised in regard to the Judgment Seat of Christ. To think that a believer would be allowed into Heaven at death and then have to await his judgment with sins still on his account is certainly inconceivable. It is contrary to the glorified condition of the believer who is absent from the body and at Home with the Lord (2 Cor. 5:6–10). We must conclude, therefore, that of necessity a transformation takes place in the believer's spiritual character at the moment he passes from the physical realm into the spiritual realm. Whether it be by confession or not (the Scriptures are silent on this point), a "making right" process must occur, which restores complete fellowship between the believer and the Lord. This does not mean that such a believer will not later be held accountable for his deeds at the Judgment Seat of Christ, but it does mean that the sin aspect has been removed.

Perhaps the most neglected aspect of the Judgment Seat of Christ has to do with punishment. The New Testament plainly reveals many forms of punishment. First Corinthians 3:15 clearly states that believers will "suffer loss" at that time. Having no "crowns" bestowed on them will be a form of punishment. The parable of the pounds (Luke 19:12–27) describes how a servant (a believer) had his pound taken away from him. This illustration speaks of how some unfruitful believers, although allowed into the millennial Kingdom, will be relegated to last place and given no authority. Having no authority will be a form of punishment. Hebrews 13:17 speaks of the Judgment Seat of Christ being "unprofitable" for those believers whose spiritual leaders have to give account of them "with grief." The sinning believer is told in Colossians 3:25 that he will receive without partiality from the hand of the Lord the consequences of the wrong that he has done. To "suffer loss" means a great deal more than most realize. Although the discipline administered at the Judgment Seat of Christ must take on a form different from that experienced by believers in this life, we must not overlook the reality of such a loss and its severity. Its severity is revealed in 2 John 8 and Revelation 3:11 where believers are told that by subsequent actions it is possible for them to lose rewards already laid up. Add to these passages those that indicate the possibility of experiencing sorrow and regret at that time, and one has to conclude that punishment will be an aspect of the Judgment Seat of Christ. Hebrews 13:17 says "grief" will be felt. First John 2:28 describes the possibility of experiencing "shame" and a desire to "shrink away from" the presence of Christ. First John 4:18 teaches that "fear" of punishment will seize those who have not been "perfected in love."

Although the process of judgment will not be a pleasant experience for many believers, the New Testament indicates that the outcome of the Judgment Seat of Christ is a different matter. The picture the New Testament gives of the believer in Heaven *after* the Judgment Seat of Christ is one of completeness and fulness of joy (Eph. 5:27; Col. 1:22; 1 Thess. 3:13; 5:23; Jude 24). The results of judgment will still be evident throughout eternity. Some believers will have varying degrees of authority, while others will have none. Some will enjoy the rewards they have won, while others will have no rewards to enjoy. The bodies of believers in Heaven vary in glory and will throughout eternity, but all are glorified, perfected bodies (1 Cor. 15:40–44). Though the results of the Judgment Seat of Christ will continue throughout eternity, the emotions of sorrow, regret and disappointment experienced during the process of judgment will certainly not remain with the believer. "When that event is over, he will enter into the purpose of Christ with fullness of joy, because he knows that the Judge of all the earth has done rightly."

The next two sections have been adapted from L. Sale-Harrison in *The Judgment Seat of Christ*.[8]

THE SERIOUSNESS OF A LIFE OF FAILURE

We have already suggested that God cannot condone sin in His children. It is a serious thing to trifle with one's liberty in Christ or to act as though liberty means license. Let us face the issue and see what it involves.

We must review: Can God condone sin in His children simply because they are members of His family? If so, then God's grace revealed in salvation gives its recipients a license to sin. This cannot be the attitude of a righteous God, even if He is our Father. We cannot become consecrated Christians unless we also hold ourselves responsible for the trust that comes with Christian citizenship; though it is quite possible for us to fail in our trust and still be Christians. To lose fellowship does not mean to lose sonship; but it certainly results in losing a reward.

To be members of the family of God means that we have accepted family responsibilities that we cannot ignore without serious loss here and hereafter.

This is what the apostle stated in 1 John 2:28: "And now, little children, abide in him; that, when he shall appear, we may have confidence, and *not be ashamed* before him at his coming."

Will the unfaithful Christian be ashamed when he meets the Lord? John suggests a positive answer, does he not? If sin has been completely atoned for and all sin's penalties removed, how can one feel ashamed? Our further discussion will give the answer.

First John 2:28 certainly reveals two things:

1. The child of God who lives a life of defeat is not cleansed from all unrighteousness.

2. As God cannot condone sin, it must therefore be reviewed at the Judgment Seat of Christ.

This brings to our minds something of the seriousness of professing to belong to the Lord, while at the same time not seeking to have fellowship with Him.

The apostle Peter further amplified this truth when he stated that judgment must begin at the house of God.

JUDGMENT BEGINS AT THE HOUSE OF GOD

"For the time is [coming] that judgment must begin at the house of God: and if it first begin at us, what shall the end be of them that obey not the gospel of God?" (1 Pet. 4:17). This verse asks, If God demands so much from the Christian, what hope has the man who refuses the gospel of Christ? The apostle said that judgment must begin at the house of God. It must begin with the Church. What does he mean by the word "judgment"?

Some would suggest that this passage was referring to the fiery trials that were to come upon the early Church, but the apostle's message reaches further than that. Did he not ask, "If it first begin at us, what shall the end be of them that obey not the gospel of God? And if the righteous scarcely be saved [saved with difficulty], where shall the ungodly and the sinner appear?" (vv. 17, 18). The apostolic writer certainly was referring to our relationship with God. *Judgment* must begin with us—*what judgment?*

Is it not true that the Holy Spirit keeps us sensitive to sin? Of course, if we grieve him, our minds become beclouded. Then His presence in us is not realized—not because He is not present but because we are not in fellowship with Him. Still He convicts us of our failure and sin. He never fails to speak to our hearts; and it is through the Word of God that He operates on the conscience. In other words, He searches us; and if we accept this operation of the Spirit and acknowledge this conviction as God Himself, we will attain only one result: the soul will immediately confess this sin, judge it and claim forgiveness.

What if my sin has injured another? Does my confession to God *alone* satisfy? No! Certainly not. I have a solemn duty to the one I have wronged. I must set it right; and if restitution is necessary, I must make it. If my course of action has injured another's reputation, I must endeavor to clear his character, or testimony, in proportion to the publicity of the injury.

I cannot remove this responsibility merely by crying to God for forgiveness, for there is no real confession unless it carries with it the determination—by God's grace—to remove the stigma that I have placed on the soul of another. Confession in such a case is, therefore, not as simple as it looks. If I have any Christian honor, I will endeavor to heal the wound that my slanderous tongue has caused. Thinking that I was in the right does not justify my exploding another Christian's reputation.

If I have grieved or injured only one person—an act that is unknown to others—the confession need go only as far as the sin has gone.

But if I do not make amends, God cannot richly bestow His blessings on me here. Furthermore, I will have to endure the "shame" of my reprehensible conduct when God exposes it at the

Judgment Seat of Christ.

The Holy Spirit today is revealing the truth of Peter's word, "Judgment must begin at the house of God." I believe that He is speaking definitely in these latter days as never before, for the greatest spiritual work done in this closing period of the Church is that of bringing Christians back to God.

Here are the words of the apostle John: "But if we walk in the light, as he is in the light, we have fellowship one with another, and the blood of Jesus Christ his Son cleanseth us from all sin. If we confess our sins, he is faithful and just to forgive us our sins, and to cleanse us from all unrighteousness" (1 John 1:7, 9).

If the positive is true, the negative is also true. What if we do not walk in the light? Are we morally cleansed? What if we do not confess our sins? Can God cleanse us from all unrighteousness?

The judicial aspect of cleansing (that which affects the standing of our salvation) is not suggested in this passage. It is the moral aspect that is brought into view. The *judicial* has to do with our saved (or lost) condition; but the *moral* is that which refers to our faithfulness (or unfaithfulness) to God—as those who are saved through the work of Calvary.

We must carefully note that the apostle John is writing to Christians and not to those outside the family of God. We again state that God cannot condone sin, even in His children. If He did, we would use the grace of God bestowed upon us as an excuse for a sinful life. A victorious life under such conditions would be well nigh impossible.

Read again 1 John 1:9: "If we confess our sins, he is faithful and just to forgive us our sins, and to cleanse us from all unrighteousness." Therefore if we do not confess our sins, that unrighteousness that has not been cleansed must be manifested (exposed) at the Judgment Seat of Christ:

> Every man's work shall be made manifest [exposed]: for the day [i.e. when the Lord comes—see 4:5] shall declare it, because it shall be revealed by fire; and the fire shall try every man's work of what sort it is. If any man's work shall be burned, he shall suffer loss: but he himself shall be saved; yet so as by [through] fire (1 Cor. 3:13, 15).

> For we must all appear before the judgment seat of Christ; that every one may receive the things done in his body, according to that he hath done, whether it be good or bad (2 Cor. 5:10).

Surely no conscientious believer can ignore either the importance of these Scriptures or the true meaning of them. The solemn message running through them all is that judgment must begin with us. And if we are unwilling to make this judgment here in our pilgrimage, it will be made for us when our pilgrimage is over.

When Paul wrote to the Colossians, he said: "Knowing that of the Lord ye shall receive the reward of the inheritance: for ye serve the Lord Christ. But he that doeth wrong shall receive for the wrong which he hath done: and there is no respect of persons" (Col. 3:24, 25).

The apostle here stated to the Christians in Colosse, "You will—at the Judgment Seat of Christ—receive for the wrong which you have done." This Scripture brings our subject to an impressive climax. It is necessary that we seek to understand it; and we will do well to take heed of its warning.

Let us repeat: "God cannot condone sin even in His children."

Some Christians are so worldly, and often grossly carnal, that one wonders how they can be happy, knowing one day they will have to give an account to God—that is, if they were ever saved.

THE BRIDE MAKING HERSELF READY

The following discussion has been adapted from *The Book of the Revelation* by Lehman Strauss.[9]

Now notice a statement concerning the Lamb's wife: "And his wife hath made herself ready. And to her was granted that she should be arrayed in fine linen, clean and white: for the fine linen is the righteousness of saints" (Rev. 19:7, 8).

Why is it stated that she has made herself ready? Is not salvation entirely of grace apart from works? The answer to these and related questions is found, in part, in the American Standard Version as well as in some other versions, where we read, ". . . the fine linen is the righteous acts of the saints." The original Greek text shows that the word "righteousness" is literally *righteousnesses* or *righteous deeds.* Here the righteous deeds of the saints are not to be confused with the righteousness of God, which is imputed to each believing sinner at the time of conversion (Rom. 3:21, 22). No sinner can work for this righteousness, as it is received only by faith. It is true of all unsaved persons that "all our righteousnesses are as filthy rags" (Isa. 64:6). But when we receive Jesus Christ as Savior and Lord, we can say, "Dressed in His righteousness alone, / Faultless to stand before the throne."

However, Revelation 19:8 refers to the righteous acts of the saints (right doing while on earth as saints). All saints will not be ready to meet Christ when He comes for His Church. Some will be ashamed at His coming. Many are guilty of committing unrighteous acts. These are unfit garments to be wearing on their wedding day. So while God has been preparing the earth for the reign of the saints, He must also prepare the saints to be presented to a prepared earth. The fact that the Lamb's wife has made herself ready suggests she was unready before. Too many Christians assume that because they are saved, they can live careless lives and still go to Heaven. It is true that when Christ appears at the Rapture, all saints of the Church Age, both living and dead, will be caught up to be with Him. But before they can reign with Him, they must face a reckoning.

Has it ever occurred to you, my Christian friend, that at the marriage of the Bride to the Lamb, each of us will be wearing the wedding garment of our own making? We must confess to our shame that the Bride is now unready for the wedding. Many carnal, selfish Christians live worldly lives, and all such must pass through the fires of the Judgment Seat of Christ before they qualify to reign with Christ. The Judgment Seat, which follows the Rapture, will not be a happy experience for every Christian. I know some of us will experience loss and shame (Rom. 14:10; 1 Cor. 3:11–15; 2 Cor. 5:10). But we *must* all appear before Christ for the final inspection and necessary readiness for the marriage.

Dr. DeHaan stated,

> In Ephesians 5:26 we are told that Christ will sanctify and cleanse His Church by the washing of water by the Word. The two words

used, "sanctify" and "cleanse," are not the same in the Greek. The word translated "cleanse" in this verse is *katharizo*, from which our English word "cathartic" is derived. God uses two methods of making us clean. One is by "sanctifying," by washing by the Word. If we refuse this method, He will give us a "cathartic," but He will have us clean. How much better to take the gentle course now than to wait until the Judgment Seat of Christ and be purged by fire!

The wedding gown, then, will be made up of the good works that remain after the testing of the Judgment Seat of Christ. Now you can see how the wife makes herself ready. It used to be customary for the bride to make her own wedding dress. When a girl met a young man and he began to court her, she would acquire a hope chest and commence to lay away lovely, clean pieces of apparel in anticipation of her wedding day. She would work diligently to prepare her own bridal gown. Christian, what are we putting in the bridal chest for that day? Of what will our wedding garments be made? The fruit of a good and godly life will make a lovely garment for that glorious occasion.

'JUDGMENT SEAT' OR 'AWARDS PODIUM'?

The remainder of this chapter is an adaptation of the article " 'Judment Seat' or 'Awards Podium' " by Dr. John A. Sproule.[10]

To suggest among evangelicals that the Bema Seat of 2 Corinthians 5:10 involves an awesome judgment of believers as well as a bestowal of rewards raises more eyebrows than the legendary Lady Godiva.

The issue is, What does the New Testament clearly teach about this Judgment Seat of Christ? To my knowledge there is no substantial work produced by those who hold to a dispensational theology, dealing with the negative aspect of the Bema Seat. In this brief section, some exegetical issues will be raised and some conclusions drawn. The two most explicit passages are 2 Corinthians 5:10 and Colossians 3:25. Primary attention will focus on the Corinthians passage.

2 CORINTHIANS 5:10

To capture the force behind the Greek text of this passage, Dr. Sproule gave an expanded literal translation. "For it is necessary that all we [believers] be made manifest before the judgment seat of Christ, in order that each one might receive back [be recompensed] for the things which he practiced through the body, whether good or evil."

The word translated "evil" (*phaulos*), contrary to the disclaimer that it means only "useless," definitely has moral connotations, and in almost every New Testament usage it is juxtaposed with *agathos* ("good") rather than some Greek word meaning "useful."

The word *komisetai* ("might receive back") deserves close examination. The verb *komizo* occurs in eight New Testament passages and in the middle voice (as in 2 Cor. 5:10). It carries the thought of "to receive" or "to receive back." Whether that which is received back is good or bad must be determined by other words in the context. Vine gives one meaning as "to receive back, recover, Matt. 25:27; Heb. 11:19; metaphorically, or requital, 2 Cor. 5:10; Col. 3:25, of 'receiving back again' by the believer at the Judgment Seat of Christ hereafter, for wrong done in this life. . . ." Significantly, the concept of *requital* is also the understanding given by Abbott-Smith for both 2 Corinthians 5:10 and Colossians 3:25.

Plummer gets to the heart of the awesomeness of 2 Corinthians 5:10 and the meaning of *komizesthai* with his comments on the *purpose* clause ("in order that each one might receive back . . ."). He wrote:

> "In order that each one may receive as his due the things done by means of his body." This corrects the false inference which might be drawn from . . . ["we all"]. We shall not be judged *en masse,* or in classes, but one by one, in accordance with individual merit. "St. Paul does not say merely that he shall receive according to what he has done in the body, but that he shall receive the things done—the very selfsame things he did; they are to be his punishment" (F. W. Robertson, *Lectures on the Epp. to the Corinthians,* p. 377). Chrys. points out that men are not much influenced by the prospect of losing

possible blessings; the dread of possible pains is more influential. . . .
In all three passages II Cor. 5:10, Eph. 6:8, Col. 3:25 . . . 'to get what
is one's own,' comes to mean 'to get as an equivalent,' 'to be
requited.' Hort (on 1 Peter 1:9) says that . . . "always in the N.T.
[*komizesthai*] means not simply to receive but to receive back, to get
what has belonged to oneself but has been lost, or promised, or kept
back, or what has come to be one's own by earning.

Similar usage of this verb is found in the LXX and the papyri.
Thus 2 Corinthians 5:10 sets forth the reason believers should
have "as their ambition" a life that is pleasing to the Lord (2 Cor.
5:9). That reason is plain: The life of every believer will one day be
appropriately opened in the presence of the Lord in order that
each believer may receive from the Lord that which is his due—
either reward or punishment or both—based upon the things
done through his body in life as a believer, whether good or bad.

This truth, however, must be viewed from the perspective of
the total teaching of Scripture. It would be inconsistent with
1 John 1:9 to imagine that sins truly confessed by a believer would
ever come to light at the Bema Seat, for such sins are forgiven
when confessed. Sproule also emphasized that a believer's salvation and eternal destiny are in no way endangered (cf. 1 Cor.
3:15), for this issue has been settled once and for all by Christ's
atoning work. A true believer can never come under the fiery
indignation or wrath of God. This means that whatever future
judgment the believer will experience it will not be some kind of
Roman *purgatory*. Christ died for the sins of men; man himself
cannot atone for sin *in any purgatorial fashion!*

Further, we cannot precisely describe what judgment a believer will receive at the Bema Seat or the time factors involved, for
the Bible is silent concerning such details. We should certainly
regard the Bema Seat as consisting of more than a "loss of reward,"
for that is hardly a matter of concern for most indolent Christians.
Further, the use of *komizesthai* in the passage forbids this understanding; that is, the idea of "receiving back or recompensing"
argues against it. It might be argued that since believers at the
Bema Seat will be *like Christ* (1 John 3:2), the loss or reward under
these conditions will be agonizingly meaningful. However, this

begs the question of how long this condition of agony would last, and would not such a sustained condition be essentially similar to a Roman purgatory? In view of the Bible's silence concerning certain details, speculations about the kind of judgment and its duration are ill-advised.)

COLOSSIANS 3:23–25

(In Colossians 3:25, Paul wrote, "But he that doeth wrong shall receive for the wrong which he hath done: and there is no respect of persons." The context has to do with the motivation of slaves in serving their masters. They are to do their work "heartily, as to the Lord [rather than for] men; knowing that [from] the Lord [they] shall receive the reward of the inheritance" (Col. 3:23, 24). Thus it seems evident that the judgment referred to in Colossians 3:25 comes from God, with Whom there is "no respect of persons," and that this judgment is yet future ("shall receive back") as the main verb in the verse indicates. The phrase, "the one who does wrong," may refer to ill-motivated and ill-treated slaves, or it may refer to unfair masters (most likely, in view of Eph. 6:5–9). However, the context of Christian slaves and Christian masters (Col. 4:1) indicates that the phrase does refer to *Christians*. Again, the main verb *komisetai* (future, middle) appears, carrying the thought of "receiving back" as established earlier.

Thus, in context Colossians 3:23–25 plainly teaches that the Lord will recompense faithful service with rewards but will also pay back wrongdoing with a requital fitting the offense. The repayment is future and, when compared with 2 Corinthians 5:10, refers evidently to the Bema Seat.)Abbott calls the phrase "the one who does wrong shall receive back that which he did wrong" *a foundational axiom* of Christianity.

CONCLUSION

1. The issue at the Bema Seat is not the eternal destiny of believers. True believers have been judged in Christ as far as eternal condemnation is concerned, and they have eternal life (John 5:24, Rom. 8:1, et al.).
2. (At the Bema Seat, believers will be rewarded for lives of

faithful service and obedience to the Word of God (1 Cor. 3:13–15). However, strong evidence indicates that believers at the Judgment Seat of Christ will suffer some kind of divine chastisement for slothful, careless lives. This involves more than simply the loss of reward. Concerning details, the Bible is silent.

3. Is the Bema Seat, therefore, a "judgment seat" or an "awards podium"? The answer: both!

THE GREAT WHITE THRONE JUDGMENT

Before I close this book, I want to become personal and lovingly point out to you that if you have never experienced the new birth you, too, will give account of yourself to God: "So then every one of us shall give account of himself to God" (Rom. 14:12).

Yes, there will be a last judgment where the unsaved will be judged and suffer the penalty decreed. This will take place at the Great White Throne Judgment. "And as it is appointed unto men once to die, but after this the judgment" (Heb. 9:27). "But the LORD shall endure for ever: he hath prepared his throne for judgment" (Ps. 9:7).

THE JUDGE

John wrote: "And I saw a great white throne, and him that sat on it. . . . And I saw the dead, small and great, stand before God" (Rev. 20:11, 12). According to the Word of God, Jesus Christ will be the judge. Jesus said, "For the Father judgeth no man, but hath committed all judgment unto the Son. . . . For as the Father hath life in himself; so hath he given to the Son to have life in himself; and hath given him authority to execute judgment also, because he is the Son of man" (John 5:22, 26, 27).

Paul said concerning Jesus Christ:

> And he commanded us to preach unto the people, and to testify that it is he which was ordained of God to be the Judge of quick and dead . . . Because he hath appointed a day, in the which he will judge the world in righteousness by that man whom he hath ordained; whereof he hath given assurance unto all men, in that he hath raised

> him from the dead. . . . I charge thee therefore before God, and the Lord Jesus Christ, who shall judge the quick and the dead at his appearing and his kingdom (Acts 10:42; 17:31; 2 Tim. 4:1).

Jesus Christ is the judge of "the quick and the dead." The word "quick" means living. In Matthew 25:31–46, we read of a future day when Christ returns to earth and judges those who are alive.

In Romans 14:10 and 2 Corinthians 5:10, the Bible speaks of a future day when those who have died in Christ and those who are caught up at the Rapture will be judged by Him at the Judgment Seat of Christ.

In Revelation 20:11–15, God spoke of a future judgment when every unsaved person will come before Jesus Christ to be judged.

THE JUDGED

Those who will be judged are called "the dead, small and great" (Rev. 20:12). These are the ones of whom it is said, "the rest of the dead lived not again until the thousand years were finished" (Rev. 20:5).

The Word of God teaches no such thing as a general judgment, when everyone who has ever lived will be judged at the same time. The Bible instead speaks of two resurrections. Daniel wrote: "And many of them that sleep in the dust of the earth shall awake, some to everlasting life, and some to shame and everlasting contempt" (Dan. 12:2). Jesus promised: "And thou shalt be blessed; for they cannot recompense thee: for thou shalt be recompensed at the resurrection of the just" (Luke 14:14). He said in John 5:28 and 29: "Marvel not at this: for the hour is coming, in the which all that are in the graves shall hear his voice, And shall come forth; they that have done good, unto the resurrection of life; and they that have done evil, unto the resurrection of damnation."

Paul said, "And have hope toward God, which they themselves also allow, that there shall be a resurrection of the dead, both of the just and unjust" (Acts 24:15).

The resurrection of life for the just to everlasting life is called the first resurrection (Rev. 20:5, 6). Christ was the firstfruits of the first resurrection (1 Cor. 15:20, 23). Then those who are saved in this Church Age, "they that are Christ's at his coming" (1 Cor. 15:23), will be resurrected at the Rapture (1 Thess. 4:16, 17). Old Testament saints will be resurrected at the conclusion of the Tribulation (Isa. 26:19; Dan. 12:1–3), as will the tribulation martyrs (Rev. 20:4).

In his book *Things to Come,* J. Dwight Pentecost summarized:

> The order of events in the resurrection program would be: (1) the resurrection of Christ as the beginning of the resurrection program (1 Cor. 15:23); (2) the resurrection of the church age saints at the rapture (1 Thess. 4:16); (3) the resurrection of the tribulation period saints (Rev. 20:3–5), together with (4) the resurrection of Old Testament saints (Dan. 12:2; Isa. 26:19) at the second advent of Christ to the earth, and finally (5) the final resurrection of the unsaved dead (Rev. 20:5, 11–14) at the end of the millennial age. The first four stages would all be included in the first resurrection or resurrection to life, inasmuch as all receive eternal life and the last would be the second resurrection, or the resurrection unto damnation, inasmuch as all receive eternal judgment at that time.

All those taking part in the first resurrection will be raised before the Millennium. Those taking part in the second resurrection will be raised after the Millennium (Rev. 20:7–15). All of the unrighteous of all ages from Cain to those who rebel during and at the close of the Millennium will stand at this great white throne to be judged. The "small and great" will be there—the beggar and the banker, the pauper and the prince, the simpleton and the scientist, the big sinners and the little sinners, rulers and subjects, the refined and the vulgar, the civilized and the barbarous—all will appear before the Judge, awaiting their eternal doom. The drunkards, the harlots, the thieves, the adulterers, the rejectors, the neglecters, the infidels, the modernists, the self-righteous will be there. The "fearful, and unbelieving, and the abominable, and murderers, and whoremongers, and sorcerers, and idolaters, and all liars" will be there (Rev. 21:8). Even though their bodies have been buried or in the depths of the sea for centuries or millennia, they will be reunited with their souls and spirits and stand before the Lord. God said in Romans 14:11: "As I live, saith the Lord, every knee shall bow to me, and every tongue shall confess to God." And in Philippians 2:10 and 11, He said: "That at the name of Jesus every knee should bow, of things in heaven, and things in earth, and things under the earth; And that every tongue should confess that Jesus Christ is Lord, to the glory of God the Father." Dr. John R. Rice commented on these verses:

> They will not love Jesus, they will not trust Him for salvation, and it will be too late for them to be saved. But the stiff knee of every rebellious and Christ-rejecting sinner will bow before Jesus in humility, and every blaspheming tongue will at that time confess that Jesus Christ is the Lord and Master that they ought to have served and loved. . . .

> The "knee" refers to the physical body. The "tongue" refers to the physical body. Resurrected sinners in bodies fresh from the graves and the sea will stand before God to be judged in the flesh for deeds done in the flesh and then to be cast, both soul and body, into Hell, the lake of fire. . . .

> The last grave will be opened in every cemetery. A thousand years before, the saints will have been raised and their graves left empty; now the remaining graves will give up their dead as spirits come out of Hell to possess them and to be judged before God.[2]

A true incident recounted some time ago in *Moody Monthly* emphasizes the unavoidable fact of the resurrection awaiting all men:

> More than a hundred years ago an infidel died in Hanover, Germany. Before his death he ordered that above his grave large slabs of granite should be placed, bound together with iron bands, and above it all a huge block weighing almost two tons. It was done. On the stone the inscription was put, "This grave is purchased for eternity; it shall never be opened." Somehow, a little poplar seed was enclosed in the mold within the tomb. God in His power caused it to sprout. A little shoot found a crevice in between the ironbound slabs. Its hidden power in the course of time broke the iron bands asunder

and moved every stone out of its original position. The whole structure [was] displaced completely and the grave [was] opened thereby. The tree still lives and waves its branches over the rent sepulcher, which the infidel declared should never be opened. It just needed a tiny seed, one of God's marvels in creation to answer the challenge of the infidel. If a tiny seed can burst open a grave, how much more can an omnipotent Lord with His omnipotent power make good His promise?[3]

THE JUDGMENT

As we have already seen, the Bible does not teach a general judgment. The Scriptures speak of seven judgments. The first three mentioned deal with believers only.

THE JUDGMENT OF THE BELIEVER'S SINS

The judgment of the believer's sin is past, deals with our justification and was accomplished for us by Christ when He suffered on the cross for our sins. At Calvary He bore the penalty of our sins: "Who his own self bare our sins in his own body on the tree" (1 Pet. 2:24). Because the believer's sins have been judged, we can joyfully sing:

> Jesus paid it all,
> All to Him I owe;
> Sin had left a crimson stain—
> He washed it white as snow.
> —*Elvina M. Hall*

Jesus promised: "Verily, verily, I say unto you, He that heareth my word, and believeth on him that sent me, hath everlasting life, and shall not come into condemnation [or judgment]; but is passed from death unto life" (John 5:24). God gave the Christian blessed assurance in Romans 8:1: "There is therefore now no condemnation to them which are in Christ Jesus." The true believer in Christ is saved and free from present condemnation and also free from fear of any future judgment at the Great White Throne.

THE JUDGMENT OF
THE BELIEVER'S SELF

The judgment of the believer's self is present, deals with our sanctification and is to be done by the believer himself. First Corinthians 11:31 is one of the most reassuring verses in the Bible: "For if we would judge ourselves, we should not be judged." If Christians would examine themselves, judge the things that are wrong in their lives and confess them to God, He would not have to judge or chasten. The Holy Spirit led John to write, "If we confess our sins, he is faithful and just to forgive us our sins, and to cleanse us from all unrighteousness" (1 John 1:9). If we do not judge ourselves, God will have to judge us, and "when we are judged, we are chastened of the Lord, that we should not be condemned with the world" (1 Cor. 11:32).

THE JUDGMENT OF
THE BELIEVER'S WORKS

The judgment of the believer's works is future, deals with our glorification, and will take place immediately after the Rapture of the Church (Rom. 14:10; 1 Cor. 4:5; 2 Cor. 5:10; 2 Tim. 4:8). This is known as the Judgment Seat of Christ, where our works as Christians will be reviewed. The faithful Christians will be rewarded; the unfaithful Christians will suffer loss (1 Cor. 3:9–15).

THE JUDGMENT OF THE NATIONS

The judgment of the nations is future and will take place at the return of Jesus Christ at the close of the Tribulation. Jesus told His disciples of that day:

> When the Son of man shall come in his glory, and all the holy angels with him, then shall he sit upon the throne of his glory: And before him shall be gathered all nations: and he shall separate them one

from another, as a shepherd divideth his sheep from the goats" (Matt. 25:31, 32).

As we read verses 33–46, we see that the passage teaches that three classes of people will be at this judgment: (1) sheep, who are saved Gentiles—those who have been saved on earth during the tribulation period between the Rapture and the revelation of Christ; (2) *goats*, who are unsaved Gentiles; and (3) *my brethren*, who are the people of Israel. The scene takes place on earth. No resurrection occurs at this judgment; no books are opened. The basis of this judgment is how people have treated the Jews, those whom Christ calls "my brethren." The good works mentioned here do not teach that the people who did them were saved by their good works, but the works are the proof of their faith and salvation. This judgment has a twofold outcome: the goats, the unsaved Gentiles, will be sent away into everlasting punishment (vv. 41, 46); and the righteous will inherit the millennial Kingdom (v. 34) and enter into life eternal (v. 46).

THE JUDGMENT OF THE JEWS

The judgment of the Jews is future and speaks of the time when the Jews will be dealt with by God. Ezekiel 20:33–38 records God's statements about this judgment. God will purge out the rebels from among the Jews during the latter part of the Tribulation. This is known as "the time of Jacob's trouble" (Jer. 30:7). Two thirds of the Jews will be purged out; the remaining one third will be saved and enter the millennial Kingdom (Zech. 13:8, 9; Rom. 11:26).

THE JUDGMENT OF THE ANGELS

The judgment of the angels is future and will take place perhaps at the time Satan is judged, which will be after the Millennium and preceding the Great White Throne Judgment (Rev. 20:10, 11). Jude wrote, "And the angels which kept not their first estate, but left their own habitation, he hath reserved in everlasting chains under darkness unto the judgment of the great day" (v. 6). These are fallen angels who followed Satan in his rebellion against God. Revelation 12:4, speaking of Satan, says: "And his tail drew the third part of the stars of heaven." A note at this verse in the Pilgrim Bible reads: *"Stars.* These are the *Angels* who followed Satan in his rebellion against God. . . ." Peter spoke of these angels: "For if God spared not the angels that sinned, but cast them down to hell, and delivered them into chains of darkness, to be reserved unto judgment" (2 Pet. 2:4). These angels have been chained in pits of darkness ("hell" in the Greek is *tartaros*) waiting for the judgment of "the great day." Other fallen angels are at large, still under the direction of Satan, making up that kingdom of evil spirits arrayed against God and Christ (Matt. 12:24–27; Eph. 2:2; 6:11, 12). Satan, who led them astray, along with them will be "cast into the lake of fire and brimstone, where the beast and the false prophet are [they had been there one thousand years and were not burned up], and shall be tormented day and night for ever and ever" (Rev. 20:10).

THE JUDGMENT OF THE GREAT WHITE THRONE

The Great White Throne Judgment is in the future and is the last judgment of mankind. We read about it in Revelation 20:11–15. God will wind up all the affairs of Heaven and earth before establishing a new heaven and a new earth. This is not a throne to determine the guilt or innocence of those who appear there. No questions will be asked—all the evidence and facts are in. This judgment will determine the sentence of those who have already been declared guilty. Jesus says of the unsaved, "He that believeth on him is not condemned: but he that believeth not is condemned already, because he hath not believed in the name of the only begotten Son of God" (John 3:18).

God brings forth His books: "The books were opened: and another book was opened, which is the book of life" (Rev. 20:12). Registering the wicked required several books, but a single book was all that was needed to register the righteous. Jesus said, "Wide is the gate, and broad is the way, that leadeth to destruction, and many there be which go in thereat: Because strait is the gate, and narrow is the way, which leadeth unto life, and few there be that find it" (Matt. 7:13, 14). Daniel 7:10 says, "The judgment was set, and the books were opened."

The Book of Life will be there only to prove to the unbelievers that their names are not in it. Many people take for granted that because their names are on a church roll, they are also listed in the Book of Life. Jesus said to His disciples, "Many will say to me in that day, Lord, Lord, have we not prophesied in thy name? and in thy name have cast out devils? and in thy name done many wonderful works? And then will I profess unto them, I never knew you: depart from me, ye that work iniquity" (Matt. 7:22, 23). Some names are written in the Book of Life (Luke 10:20; Phil. 4:3), and some are not (Rev. 13:8; 17:8; 20:15). Only those whose names are in this book go to Heaven (Rev. 21:27). My friend, ask yourself this question:

> Is my name written there
> On the page white and fair?
> In the book of Thy kingdom,
> Is my name written there?

If you are unsure, as Peter instructed, "Give diligence to make your calling and election sure . . ." (2 Pet. 1:10). "Believe on the Lord Jesus Christ, and thou shalt be saved" (Acts 16:31). When you repent of your sins and receive Jesus Christ as your personal Savior and Lord, you can be sure, and then you can rejoice, because your name is written in Heaven" (Luke 10:20). Then you can sing:

> Yes, my name's written there
> On the page white and fair;
> In the book of Thy kingdom,
> Yes, my name's written there!
> —*Mary A. Kidder*

Certain other books will also be opened. These contain an exact record of all that has happened in each sinner's life. Everyone will be judged "according to their works" (Rev. 20:12, 13). God is fair and just in His judgments. God is an accurate bookkeeper, and He has stated: "Be sure your sin will find you out"

(Num. 32:23). These books will reveal the unrighteous thoughts and deeds, the neglected opportunities and the degree of sinfulness and guilt of every unsaved person.

The Word of God teaches degrees of punishment. Jesus said to some cities that had rejected Him, "It shall be more tolerable for Tyre and Sidon at the day of judgment, than for you. . . . It shall be more tolerable for the land of Sodom, in the day of judgment, than for thee" (Matt. 11:22, 24). He also said,

> And that servant, which knew his lord's will, and prepared not himself, neither did according to his will, shall be beaten with many stripes. But he that knew not, and did commit things worthy of stripes, shall be beaten with few stripes. For unto whomsoever much is given, of him shall be much required: and to whom men have committed much, of him they will ask the more (Luke 12:47, 48).

Christ spoke of the scribes and said of them, "The same shall receive greater damnation" (Luke 20:47). The difference in degrees will not be in the length of punishment but in the severity of punishment.

Words Will Be Judged. Jesus said, "But I say unto you, that every idle word that men shall speak, they shall give account thereof in the day of judgment. For by thy words thou shalt be justified, and by thy words thou shalt be condemned (Matt. 12:36, 37). Jude talked about the same kind of judgment:

> And Enoch also, the seventh from Adam, prophesied of these, saying, Behold, the Lord cometh with ten thousands of his saints, to execute judgment upon all, and to convince all that are ungodly among them of all their ungodly deeds which they have ungodly committed, and of all their hard speeches which ungodly sinners have spoken against him (Jude 14, 15).

Actions Will Be Judged. The Bible says, "for the LORD is a God of knowledge, and by him *actions are weighed*" (1 Sam. 2:3). King Belshazzar was told by God, "Thou art weighed in the balances, and art found wanting" (Dan. 5:27). Every sinner at this judgment will be "found wanting."

Works Will Be Judged. Twice in this passage (Rev. 20:12, 13) God says people will be judged "according to their works." The thought of God judging every person according to his works is found as many as forty-two times in the Bible (see Ps. 62:12; Prov. 24:12; Isa. 3:11; Jer. 17:10; 32:19; Ezek. 7:3, 27; Rom. 2:6; Gal. 6:7; 2 Tim. 4:14; Rev. 2:23; 18:6). At this judgment every lost sinner will experience the truth of these words: "Be not deceived; God is not mocked: for whatsoever a man soweth, that shall he also reap" (Gal. 6:7).

Secret Things Will Be Judged. Ecclesiastes 12:14 says: "For God shall bring every work into judgment, with every secret thing, whether it be good, or whether it be evil." Paul said, "In the day when God shall judge the secrets of men by Jesus Christ according to my gospel" (Rom. 2:16). Jesus said, "For there is nothing covered, that shall not be revealed; neither hid, that shall not be known" (Luke 12:2). Think of the sins hidden in the hearts of millions of people. People think they are hidden, but at this judgment everything will be exposed; every skeleton will come out of the closet.

Every Work Will Be Judged. Ecclesiastes 12:14 says, "For God shall bring every work into judgment." The writer of Hebrews stated, "Neither is there any creature that is not manifest in his sight: but all things are naked and opened unto the eyes of him with whom we have to do" (Heb. 4:13). Yes, the sinner's words, actions, works, secrets—all will be open to the eyes of Jesus Christ.

William R. Newell, in his great book, *Romans Verse by Verse,* as he was commenting on chapter 2 of Romans, gave seven principles of God's judgment:

1. God's judgment is according to truth (verse 2).
2. [God's judgment is] according to accumulated guilt (verse 5).
3. [God's judgment is] according to works (verse 6).
4. [God's judgment is] without respect of persons (verse 11).
5. [God's judgment is] according to performance, not knowledge (verse 13).
6. God's judgment reaches the secrets of the heart (verse 16).
7. [God's judgment is] according to reality, not religious profession (verses 17–29).[4]

THE SENTENCE

The sentence proclaimed at this judgment is revealed in Revelation 20:14 and 15: "And death and hell were cast into the lake of fire. This is the second death. And whosoever was not found written in the book of life was cast into the lake of fire." "Death" here refers to the grave, which received the body; "hell" here is a translation of the Greek word *hades*. Man is body, soul and spirit (1 Thess. 5:23). Only the body goes to the grave, never the soul and spirit. The soul and spirit of an unsaved person go immediately to *Hades* at the time of death. (See Luke 16:22, 23. "Hell" there in the Greek is *hades*.)

People have been much confused about Hell because three different Greek words have been translated by the same English word in the King James Version of the Bible. The three Greek words are *tartaros, hades* and *gehenna*, which have all been translated by the one word "hell."

The word *tartaros* occurs only once in the New Testament: "God spared not the angels that sinned, but cast them down to hell [*tartaros*], and delivered them into chains of darkness, to be reserved unto judgment" (2 Pet. 2:4). *Tartaros* is the place of confinement for the angels that sinned until Judgment Day.

The word *hades* occurs eleven times in the New Testament, ten times translated "hell" (Matt. 11:23; 16:18; Luke 10:15; 16:23; Acts 2:27, 31; Rev. 1:18; 6:8; 20:13, 14) and one time translated "grave" (1 Cor. 15:55). Thayer defines *hades* as "the infernal regions, the common receptacle of disembodied spirits." Although Hades has torment, it is not the final abode of the unsaved. Hades will one day deliver up the dead; they will be judged; and then they will be cast into the Lake of Fire.

Gerald L. Stover gave a truly helpful explanation of *hades*:

1. The Hebrew word is *Sheol*, appearing 65 times in the Old Testament. Its New Testament equivalent is the Greek, *Hades*, which appears 11 times. That they are to be identified as referring to the same place is proven by comparing Psalm 16:10 with Acts 2:31.

2. That these words are place names, referring to a locality, is an

absolute certainty. They refer to the unseen world of disembodied spirits.

3. In the Old Testament and up to the time of the atoning work of Jesus Christ in terms of death and resurrection it would seem that the spirits of the lost and the saved went to Sheol or Hades, the two classes being separated by a vast gulf in the unseen world (Luke 16:19–31). . . . The portion of Hades occupied by the saints in the intermediate state is referred to as *Abraham's bosom* (Luke 16:22) and *paradise* (Luke 23:43).

4. Throughout the Old and New Testaments Sheol and Hades receives the spirits of the lost. After the death of our Lord Jesus Christ and His resurrection, we do not read of a single believer going to Hades. The teaching of the New Testament dispensation is summed up in such words as: "We are confident, I say, and willing rather to be absent from the body, and to be present with the Lord" (II Corinthians 5:8). "For I am in a strait betwixt two, having a desire to depart, and to be with Christ; which is far better" (Philippians 1:23).

If we compare Psalm 68:18 with Ephesians 4:7–11 it is interesting that when Christ ascended into Heaven, He is first of all described as descending into the lower parts of the earth and leading captive to Himself a multitude of persons described in terms of captivity— these He led into Heaven itself. Evidently the saints confined for the while to the blessed part of Sheol or Hades, were delivered by the triumphant Christ and led safely to Heaven at His ascension. Thus no Christian of this dispensation goes to Hades at death. The body goes into the grave and the spirit is released into the presence of the Lord.

Our passage in Revelation 20:12, 13, described then, the resurrection of the wicked dead. They live again in the body, the graves and Hades surrendering their victims and thus body, soul and spirit are united for judgment.[5]

The word *gehenna* occurs twelve times in the New Testament (Matt. 5:22, 29, 30; 10:28; 18:9; 23:15, 33; Mark 9:43, 45, 47; Luke

12:5; James 3:6). Eleven of the twelve references are the words of Jesus Christ Himself. Harold J. Berry wrote concerning this word:

> Southeast of Jerusalem there was a valley known as the "valley of the son of Hinnom" (Joshua 15:8). It was also referred to as "Gehenna" from the Hebrew word ge-*hinnom,* which means "valley of Hinnom." During Old Testament times there were children offered to Moloch in this valley (II Chron. 33:1–6; Jer. 7:31). Later, after such heathen practices were stopped, the Jews used the valley to dispose of their rubbish, as well as the bodies of dead animals and unburied criminals. To consume all of this, a fire known as the "Gehenna of fire" burned continuously. To be in the "gehenna of fire" would be the most excruciating torment that the human mind could imagine; thus, Christ used this known place with its gnawing worms and burning fires to teach truths about the unknown place— the final abode of those who reject Him as Saviour.

There are those who do not believe in a literal Hell. God's Word definitely teaches "the wicked shall be turned into hell, and all the nations that forget God" (Ps. 9:17). Twice in verses 14 and 15 of Revelation 20, God said that the wicked were "cast into the lake of fire." People ask how a human body can live in a lake of fire without being burned up in a few minutes. In the second resurrection God will give to the unsaved new bodies. They will be made of a composition that will be able to endure the fire without being consumed. God kept the three Hebrew children from burning up in the fire, and He will keep the bodies of the unsaved from burning up for all eternity. What a terrifying thought! Charles H. Spurgeon believed in an eternal Hell and spoke to his hearers:

> But, in Hell there is no hope. They have not even the hope of dying— the hope of being annihilated. They are forever—forever—forever— lost! On every chain in Hell, there is written "forever." In the fires there blazes out the word "forever." Up above their heads, they read "forever." Their eyes are galled, and their hearts are pained with the thought that it is "forever." Oh! if I could tell you tonight that Hell would one day be burned out, and that those who were lost might be saved, there would be a jubilee in Hell at the very thought of it. But

it cannot be—it is "forever" they are "cast into utter darkness."[7]

May these words, written by J. A. Brown, be used to convict every unsaved man and woman, boy and girl:

WHEN I STAND BEFORE THE JUDGMENT BAR
In a day that is not far,
At the blazing judgment bar,
Even now the awful summons I can hear;
I must meet the mighty God,
I must face His holy Word,
I must stand before the judgment bar.

I must meet each broken vow,
That I hold so lightly now,
Every heartache I have caused, each sigh, each tear;
Things that time cannot erase,
I must meet them face to face,
When I stand before the judgment bar.

Every secret lust and thought
There shall be to judgment brought,
When the Lord in all His glory shall appear;
All the deeds of darkest night
Shall come out to greet the light
When I stand before the judgment bar.

I must meet my cankered gold,
For whose greed my life was sold,
It shall mock me in the Judgment's lurid glare,
Saying ye have sold for naught,
All the Saviour's blood had bought,
And you stand before the judgment bar.

Oh, my record will be there,
Be its pages dark or fair,
When I stand before the judgment bar;
When the books shall open lie,

In that morning bye and bye,
Oh, my record! Oh, my record will be there!

Let me turn and seek the Lord,
Let me trust His holy Word,
Let me bow and call upon Him while He's near;
Then when I my record face,
He will answer in my place
When I stand before the judgment bar.

Hell stands waiting for every person outside Christ, yet Christ also stands waiting for every person outside Hell. Jesus Christ made this wonderful promise: "Verily, verily, I say unto you, He that heareth my word, and believeth on him that sent me, hath everlasting life, and shall not come into condemnation; but is passed from death unto life" (John 5:24). He says if you hear His Word, believe on Him, receive Him as your personal Savior and Lord, you "shall not come into condemnation." God also promised in Romans 8:1, "There is therefore now no condemnation [judgment] to them which are in Christ Jesus." The person who is saved, who is in Christ Jesus, will never have to stand at the Great White Throne Judgment. If you are unsaved, if you are not in Christ, trust Him now before it is too late.

INTRODUCTION

1. Leonard Ravenhill, *Meat for Men* (Minneapolis: Bethany House Publications, 1979), pp. 14, 15.
2. John A. Sproule, " 'Judgment Seat' or 'Awards Podium,' " *Spire*, 113 (1984): 3.
3. John F. Walvoord, *The Return of the Lord* (Grand Rapids: Dunham, 1955), p. 119.
4. W. Myrddin Lewis, *Hidden Mysteries* (Glasgow: By the author, 1965), p. 87. Used by permission.
5. J. Dwight Pentecost, *Prophecy for Today* (Grand Rapids: Zondervan Publishing House, 1961), p. 150.
6. Saint Augustine, *The Preachers' Homiletical Commentary* (Grand Rapids: Baker Book House, 1981), p. 472.
7. A. W. Tozer, *The Tozer Pulpit*, vol. 8 (Harrisburg: Christian Publications, Inc., 1981), pp. 99, 106.
8. Sproule, p. 5.

CHAPTER 1

1. W. E. Grindstaff, *Ways to Win* (Nashville: Broadman Press, 1957), p. 117.
2. Arthur Pridham, *Notes and Reflections on the Epistle to the Romans* (Atlanta: The Granary, 1977), pp. 408–9.
3. John Linton, *Tears in Heaven and Other Sermons* (Philadelphia: Westbrook, 1942), pp. 14, 15.
4. Isaac M. Haldeman, "The Judgment Seat of Christ," in *Great Gospel Sermons,* 1:91. Used by permission of Fleming H. Revell.
5. Frederick L. Brooks, *Prophetic Glimpses* (Findlay, Ohio: Fundamental Truth Publishers), pp. 63, 64.
6. Philip Hughes, *Paul's Second Epistle to the Corinthians* (Grand Rapids: William B. Eerdmans Publishing Company, 1962), p. 180.
7. Robert T. Ketcham, *Sermons by Ketcham,* vol. 2: *Why Was Christ a Carpenter? and Other Sermons* (Des Plaines, Ill.: Regular Baptist Press, 1966), p. 136.

8. F. E. Marsh, *The Discipler's Manual* (Grand Rapids: Kregel Publications, 1980), p. 367. Used by permission of Kregel Publications.

9. Graham Scroggie, quoted in Keith L. Brooks, *Prophecy Answered* (Westchester, Ill.: Good News Publishers, 1960), pp. 61, 62. Used by permission of Good News Publishers/Crossway Books.

10. Roy L. Laurin, *Life Endures* (Grand Rapids: Kregel Publications, 1985), p. 106. Used by permission of Kregel Publications.

11. Theodore H. Epp, *Present Labor and Future Rewards* (Lincoln, Neb.: Back to the Bible, 1969), p. 24. Reprinted by permission of The Good News Broadcasting Association, Inc. All rights reserved.

12. W. H. Griffith Thomas, quoted in Robert T. Ketcham, *Sermons by Ketcham*, vol. 2: *Why Was Christ a Carpenter? and Other Sermons,* p. 147.

13. Ketcham, pp. 147–48.

14. H. H. Savage, "What God Will Do with the Unfaithful," *Founder's Week Messages* (Chicago: Moody Press, 1962), pp. 48, 50.

15. Ibid., p. 51.

16. J. A. Seiss, *The Apocalypse* (Grand Rapids: Kregel Publications, 1987), p. 479. Used by permission of Kregel Publications.

CHAPTER 2

1. John F. Walvoord, *The Return of the Lord* (Grand Rapids: Dunham, 1955), p. 119.

2. W. Myrddin Lewis, *Hidden Mysteries* (Glasgow: By the author, 1965), p. 87. Used by permission.

3. Isaac M. Haldeman, "The Judgment Seat of Christ," in *Great Gospel Sermons,* 1:93, 94. Used by permission of Fleming H. Revell.

4. Lewis, p. 87.

5. J. Dwight Pentecost, *Things to Come* (Grand Rapids: Dunham, 1958), pp. 222–23. Used by permission.

6 . E. Schuyler English, "The Church and the Tribulation" in *Prophetic Truth Unfolding Today,* p. 31.

7. Pentecost, pp. 225–26.

8. F. E. Marsh, *Fully Furnished* (London: Pickering & Inglis, 1924), p. 382.

9. Ibid., p. 390.

10. Lehman Strauss, *God's Plan for the Future* (Grand Rapids: Zondervan Publishing House, 1964), p. 115. Used by permission.

11. Keith L. Brooks, *Prophecy Answered* (Westchester, Ill.: Good News Publishers/Crossway Books, 1960), pp. 60–62. Used by permission of Good News Publishers/Crossway Books, Westchester, Illinois 60153.

12. M. R. DeHaan, *The Judgment Seat of Christ* (Grand Rapids: Radio Bible Class, 1951), p. 21.

13. Theodore Epp, *Present Labor and Future Rewards* (Lincoln, Neb.: Back to the Bible, 1960), p. 75. Reprinted by permission of the Good News Broadcasting Association, Inc. All rights reserved.

14. Lehman Strauss, *We Live Forever* (Neptune, N.J.: Loizeaux Brothers, 1947), pp. 81, 82. Used by permission of Loizeaux Brothers, Inc.

15. Emery H. Bancroft, *Christian Theology* (Grand Rapids: Zondervan Publishing House, 1949), p. 361. Used by permission of Zondervan Publishing House.

16. Haldeman, pp. 85–87. Used by permission of Fleming H. Revell.

17. Donald G. Barnhouse, *Expositions of Bible Doctrines,* vol. 9, *God's Discipline,* (Philadelphia: The Evangelical Foundation, 1964), pp. 195, 198.

18. W. H. Griffith Thomas, quoted in Robert T. Ketcham, *Sermons by Ketcham,* vol. 2: *Why Was Christ a Carpenter? and Other Sermons* (Des Plaines, Ill.: Regular Baptist Press, 1966), p. 147.

19. Lewis, pp. 86, 88, 89.

20. John H. Linton, *Tears in Heaven and Other Sermons* (Philadelphia: Westbrook, 1942), pp. 13–16.

21. Ibid. pp. 23, 24.

22. H. H. Savage, "What God Will Do with the Unfaithful," *Founder's Week Messages* (Chicago: Moody Press, 1962), pp. 55, 49.

23. L. Sale-Harrison, *The Judgment Seat of Christ* (New York: Sale-Harrison Publications, 1938), pp. 42, 51–53, 55.

24. John R. Rice, *Tears in Heaven* (Murfreesboro, Tenn.: Sword of the Lord Publishers, 1941), pp. 13–16. Used by permission of Sword of the Lord.

25. S. Franklin Logsdon, *Profiles of Prophecy* (Grand Rapids: Zondervan Publishing House, 1964), pp. 26, 28, 29.

26. F. E. Marsh, *The Discipler's Manual* (Grand Rapids: Kregel Publications, 1980), p. 367. Used by permission of Kregel Publications.

27. Robert T. Ketcham, *Sermons by Ketcham*, vol. 2: *Why Was Christ a Carpenter? and Other Sermons* (Des Plaines, Ill.: Regular Baptist Press, 1966), pp. 127–28.

28. Ibid., pp. 144–47.

29. Herbert Lockyer, "The Advent and Youth," *Prophetic Witness,* March 1969, pp. 55–56.

30. Ibid.

31. Kenneth F. Dodson, *The Prize of the Upcalling* (Grand Rapids: Baker Book House, 1969), pp. 86–88. Used by permission.

32. Linton, p. 35.

CHAPTER 3

1. The New Scofield Reference Bible, 1 Corinthians 3:14 (note).

2. F. A. Tatford, *God's Program of the Ages* (Grand Rapids: Kregel Publications, 1967), p. 73. Used by permission of Kregel Publications.

CHAPTER 4

1. L. Sale-Harrison, *The Judgment Seat of Christ* (New York: Sale-Harrison Publications, 1938), pp. 69–87.

CHAPTER 5

1. John F. MacArthur, Jr., *Marks of a True Believer* (Chicago: Moody Press, n.d.), pp. 35, 36.

2. John F. MacArthur, Jr., *Good News Broadcaster,* September 1981, p. 28.

3. Wayne Sutton, "Justification and the Judgment Seat of Christ" (M.Div. thesis, Grace Theological Seminary, 1982), p. 34.

4. Samuel L. Hoyt, "The Negative Aspects of the Christian's Judgment," *Bibliotheca Sacra,* 137 (June 1980): 131.

5. John Linton, *Tears in Heaven and Other Sermons* (Philadelphia: Westbrook, 1942), pp. 9–35.

6. Zane C. Hodges, *Grace in Eclipse* (Dallas: Rendencion Viva, 1985), pp. 50–55, 78–80. Used by permission of Redencion Viva.

7. Thomas M. Meachum, "The Judgment Seat of Christ," *Biblical Viewpoint,* 11 (April 1977): 64, 69, 70–73. Used by permission of Bob Jones University.

8. L. Sale-Harrison, *The Judgment Seat of Christ* (New York: Sale-Harrison, 1938), pp. 44, 47–55.

9. Lehman Strauss, *The Book of the Revelation* (Neptune, N.J.: Loizeaux Brothers 1964), pp. 319–21. Used by permission of Loizeaux Brothers, Inc., Neptune, New Jersey.

10. John A. Sproule, " 'Judgment Seat' or 'Awards Podium,' " *Spire,* 113 (1984): 3–5.

CHAPTER 6

1. J. Dwight Pentecost, *Things to Come* (Grand Rapids: Dunham, 1958), p. 411. Used by permission of the publisher.

2. John R. Rice, *The Last Judgment of the Unsaved Dead* (Murfreesboro, Tenn.: Sword of the Lord Publishers, 1943), pp. 10, 12. Used by permission of Sword of the Lord.

3. *Moody Monthly,* quoted by A. H. Yetter, "The Resurrection of the Unbelieving Dead," *Christian Victory,* November 1970, pp. 38–39.

4. William R. Newell, *Romans Verse by Verse* (Chicago: Moody Press, 1938), p. 54.

5. Gerald L. Stover, *Truth for Tomorrow* (Denver: Baptist Publications, 1966), pp. 85, 86. Used by permission Accent Publications.

6. Harold J. Berry, "Which Hell Is Eternal?" quoted in Theodore H. Epp, *Practical Studies in Revelation,* vol. 2, (Lincoln, Neb.: Good News Broadcasting Association, Inc., 1969), p. 450. Reprinted by permission of the Good News Broadcasting Association, Inc. All rights reserved.

7. Charles H. Spurgeon, quoted by Carl G. Johnson, *Ready for Anything,* p. 80.

Anderson, Walter E. "The 'Receiving' of II Corinthians 5:10: The Believer's Judgment." M.Div. thesis, Grace Theological Seminary, 1983.

Bancroft, Emery H. *Christian Theology.* Grand Rapids: Zondervan Publishing House, 1949.

Barackman, Floyd H. *Practical Christian Theology.* Old Tappan, N.J.: Fleming H. Revell, 1984.

Barnhouse, Donald G. *Exposition of Bible Doctrines.* vol. 9: *God's Discipline.* Philadelphia: The Evangelical Foundation, 1964.

Berry, Harold J. "Which Hell Is Eternal?" Quoted in Theodore H. Epp, *Practical Studies in Revelation,* p. 450. Lincoln, Neb.: Back to the Bible, 1969.

Blackstone, W. E. *Jesus Is Coming.* New York: Fleming H. Revell, 1908.

Brooks, Frederick L. *Prophetic Glimpses.* Findlay, Ohio: Fundamental Truth Publishers, 1939.

Brooks, Keith L. *Prophecy Answered.* Westchester, Ill.: Good News Publishers, 1960.

Criswell, W. A. *Expository Sermons on Revelation.* Grand Rapids: Zondervan Publishing House, 1962.

Dahlin, John. *Prophetic Truth for Today.* Minneapolis: Beacon Publications, 1961.

DeHaan, M. R. *The Judgment Seat of Christ.* Grand Rapids: Radio Bible Class, n.d.

Dodson, Kenneth F. *The Prize of the Up-Calling.* Grand Rapids:

Baker Book House, 1969.

Duncan, Homer. *Prepare Now for the Second Coming of Christ.* Lubbock, Tex: Missionary Crusader, n.d.

English, E. Schuyler. "The Church and the Tribulation." Quoted in Charles Feinberg, ed. *Prophetic Truth Unfolding Today*, p. 31. Westwood, N.J.: Fleming H. Revell, 1968.

Epp, Theodore H. *Practical Studies in Revelation.* 2 vols. Lincoln, Neb: Back to the Bible, 1969.

―――. *Present Labor and Future Rewards.* Lincoln, Neb.: Back to the Bible, 1969.

Feinberg, Charles L. *Focus on Prophecy.* Westwood, N.J.: Fleming H. Revell, 1964.

―――. *Prophecy and the Seventies.* Chicago: Moody Press, 1971.

―――. ed. *Prophetic Truth Unfolding Today.* Westwood, N.J.: Fleming H. Revell, 1968.

Greene, Oliver B. *Bible Prophecy.* Greenville, S.C.: The Gospel Hour, Inc., 1970.

Grindstaff, W. E. *Ways to Win.* Nashville, Tenn.: Broadman Press, 1957.

Gromacki, Robert Glenn. *Are These the Last Days?* Westwood, N.J.: Fleming H. Revell, 1970.

Haldeman, Isaac M. *Great Gospel Sermons.* Vol. 1. New York: Fleming H. Revell, 1949.

Henry, Matthew. *Matthew Henry's Commentary.* 5 vols. Westwood, N.J.: Fleming H. Revell, n.d.

Hitchcock, Floyd. *Lectures on the Revelation.* Springfield, Mo.: Johnson Print Shop, n.d.

Hodges, Zane C. *Grace in Eclipse.* Dallas: Redencion Viva, 1985.

Hough, Robert Ervin. *The Christian after Death.* Chicago: Moody Press, 1947.

Hoyt, Herman A. *The End Times.* Chicago: Moody Press, 1969.

Hoyt, Samuel L. "The Negative Aspects of the Christian's Judgment." *Bibliotheca Sacra,* 137 (April–June) 1980: 131.

Hughes, Philip. *The New International Commentary of the New Testament.* Grand Rapids: William B. Eerdmans Publishing Company, 1962.

Jamieson, Robert; Fausset, A. R.; and Brown, David. *A Commentary Critical, Experimental and Practical on the Old and New Testaments.* 2 vols. Grand Rapids: William B. Eerdmans Publishing Company, 1948.

Johnson, Carl G. *Ready for Anything.* Minneapolis: Bethany Fellowship, 1968.

Ketcham, Robert T. *Sermons by Ketcham.* Vol. 2: *Why Was Christ a Carpenter? and Other Sermons.* Des Plaines, Ill.: Regular Baptist Press, 1966.

Kurtz, Edward Cuyler. *And Behold, the Camels Were Coming.* Grand Rapids: Zondervan Publishing House, 1941.

Larkin, Clarence. *The Book of Revelation.* Philadelphia: Clarence Larkin, Estate, 1919.

Laurin, Roy L. *Life Endures.* Grand Rapids: Kregel Publications, 1985.

Lewis, W. Myrddin. *Hidden Mysteries.* Glasgow: By the Author, 1965.

Linton, John. *Tears in Heaven and Other Sermons.* Philadelphia: Westbrook, 1942.

Logsdon, S. Franklin. *Profiles of Prophecy.* Grand Rapids: Zondervan Publishing House, 1964.

Ludwigson, R. *Bible Prophecy Notes.* By the Author, 1951.

Marsh, F. E. *The Discipler's Manual.* Grand Rapids: Kregel Publications, 1980.

———. *Fully Furnished.* London: Pickering & Inglis, 1924.

MacArthur, Jr., John F. *Good News Broadcaster,* September 1981, p. 28.

———. *Marks of a True Believer.* Chicago: Moody Press, n.d.

Meachum, Thomas M. "The Judgment Seat of Christ." *Biblical Viewpoint* 11 (April 1977): 64, 69, 70–73.

Moody Monthly. Quoted in A. H. Yetter, "The Resurrection of the Unbelieving Dead." *Christian Victory,* November 1970, pp. 38, 39.

Newell, William R. *The Book of the Revelation.* Chicago: Scripture Press, 1967.

———. *Romans Verse by Verse.* Chicago: Moody Press, 1938.

Olford, Stephen F. "The Judgment Seat of Christ." *Prophecy and the Seventies.* Chicago: Moody Press, 1971.

Pache, Rene. *The Future Life.* Translated by Helen I. Needham. Chicago: Moody Press, 1962.

Panton, D. M. *The Judgment Seat of Christ.* Miami Springs, Fla.: Conley & Schoettle Publishing Company, Inc., 1984.

Pentecost, J. Dwight, *Prophecy for Today.* Grand Rapids: Zondervan Publishing House, 1961.

———. *Things to Come.* Grand Rapids: Dunham, 1958.

Pink, A. W. *The Redeemer's Return.* Swengel, Pa.: Bible Truth Depot, 1918.

Pridham, Arthur. *Notes and Reflections on the Epistle to the Romans.* Atlanta: The Granary, 1977.

Ravenhill, Leonard. *Meat for Men.* Minneapolis: Bethany House Publications, 1979.

Rice, John R. *Tears in Heaven.* Murfreesboro, Tenn.: Sword of the Lord Publications, 1941.

The Last Judgment of the Unsaved Dead. Murfreesboro, Tenn.: Sword of the Lord Publications, [1943].

Rosscup, James E. "Paul's Teaching on the Christian's Future Reward." Postgraduate thesis, The University of Aberdeen, 1976.

Sale-Harrison, L. *The Judgment Seat of Christ.* New York: Sale-Harrison Publications, 1938.

Savage, H. H. "What God Will Do with the Unfaithful." *Founder's Week Messages.* Chicago: Moody Press, 1962.

Scofield, C. I. ed. The New Scofield Reference Bible. New York: Oxford, 1967.

———. *Prophecy Made Plain.* London: Pickering & Inglis, n.d.

Scott, Walter. *Exposition of the Revelation of Jesus Christ.* London: Pickering & Inglis, n.d.

Scroggie, Graham. Quoted in Keith L. Brooks, *Prophecy Answered,* pp. 61, 62. Westchester, Ill.: Good News Publishers, 1960.

Seiss, J. A. *The Apocalypse.* Grand Rapids: Kregel Publications, 1987.

Smith, J. B. *A Revelation of Jesus Christ.* Scottdale, Pa.: Mennonite Publishing House, 1961.

Sproule, John A. " 'Judgment Seat' or 'Awards Podium.' " *Spire* 113: (1984), 3–5.

Saint Augustine. *The Preachers' Homiletical Commentary,* Grand Rapids: Baker Book House, 1981.

Stanton, Gerald B. *Kept from the Hour.* Grand Rapids: Zondervan Publishing House, 1956.

Stover, Gerald A. *Truth for Tomorrow.* Denver: Accent Publications, 1966.

Strauss, Lehman. *The Book of the Revelation.* Neptune, N.J.: Loizeaux Brothers, 1964.

———. *God's Plan for the Future.* Grand Rapids: Zondervan Publishing House, 1965.

———. *We Live Forever.* Neptune, N.J.: Loizeaux Brothers, 1947.

Sutton, Wayne. "Justification and the Judgment Seat of Christ." M.Div. thesis, Grace Theological Seminary, 1982.

Talbot, Louis T. *The Revelation of Jesus Christ.* Grand Rapids: William B. Eerdmans Publishing Company, 1937.

————. *God's Plan of the Ages.* Grand Rapids: William B. Eerdmans Publishing Company, 1936.

Tatford, Frederick A. *God's Program of the Ages.* Grand Rapids: Kregel Publications, 1967.

Thomas, W. H. Griffith. Quoted in Robert T. Ketcham, *Sermons by Ketcham.* Vol. 2: *Why Was Christ a Carpenter? and Other Sermons,* p. 147. Des Plaines, Ill.: Regular Baptist Press, 1966.

Tozer, A. W. *The Tozer Pulpit.* Vol. 8. Harrisburg: Christian Publications, Inc., 1981.

Trench, Richard C. *Synonyms of the New Testament.* Grand Rapids: William B. Eerdmans Publishing Company, 1948.

Tweeddale, William Frank. *An Examination of the Judgment Seat in II Corinthians 5:10.* B.Div. thesis, Grace Theological Seminary, 1957.

Walvoord, John F. *The Return of the Lord.* Grand Rapids: Dunham, 1955.

Wilmington, H. L. *The King Is Coming.* Wheaton, Ill.: Tyndale House Publishers, 1973.

Wood, Leon J. *The Bible and Future Events.* Grand Rapids: Zondervan Publishing House, 1973.

————. *Is the Rapture Next?* Grand Rapids: Zondervan Publishing House, [1956].

Woychuk, N. A. *For All Eternity.* New York: Books, Inc., 1955.